THE ORDEAL OF SOUTHSEA CASTLE

A. L. BOXELL

Tricorn Books

www.tricornbooks.co.uk

Tricorn Books

The Ordnance of Southsea Castle

Design © 131 Design Ltd
www.131design.org

A. L. Boxell has asserted his right under the
Copyright, Design and Patents Act 1988 to be identified
as the author of this work.

This book is sold subject to the conditions that it shall not
by way of trade or otherwise, be lent, resold, hired out or
otherwise circulated without the publishers's prior consent in any
form of binding or cover other than that in which it is published
and without a similar condition including this condition being
imposed on the subsequent purchaser.

ISBN 978-0-9562498-4-5
Published 2010 by Tricorn Books,
a trading name of 131 Design Ltd.
131 High Street, Old Portsmouth, PO1 2HW

www.tricornbooks.co.uk

Printed and bound in Great Britain by
MPG Biddles Ltd

BOOK CONTENTS

Frontispiece and Title Page

Page i	Foreword
Page ii	Acknowledgements
Page iii – iv	Abbreviations used in the text
Page v	Introduction
Page vi	Plan of the castle, showing positions of guns
Page vii	Nomenclature. Parts of a gun

PART ONE

Pages 1 – 48	Photographs and descriptions of guns 1 – 13
Page 49	Royal Ciphers used by Queen Victoria
Pages 50 – 68	Photographs and descriptions of guns 14 – 18
Page 69	'Bushing the Vent'
Pages 70 – 106	Photographs and descriptions of guns 19 – 30
Page 107	Biographies. Sir Joseph Whitworth and Baron W.G. Armstrong
Pages 108 – 119	Photographs and descriptions of guns 31 – 36

PART TWO

Pages 120 -121	Carronades
Pages 122 – 123	Royal Brass Foundry
Page 124	Gun metals. Brass, Bronze and Iron
Pages 125 – 133	Ignition Systems for gunpowder
Pages 134 – 139	Glossary of terms
Pages 140 – 144	Bibliography

Best wishes

Tony Boxall

THE ORDNANCE OF SOUTHSEA CASTLE.

FOREWORD

I remember my first visit to Southsea Castle as a schoolboy in the early 1970s and being fascinated by both the fortification and its guns. Little did I realise it then that years later I would be fortunate enough to be involved professionally with some of the latter as Curator of Artillery for Royal Armouries and based at another local fortification, Fort Nelson upon Portsdown Hill. Currently, Royal Armouries has four guns on loan at Southsea Castle under the care of Portsmouth City Council and it is my enviable task of visiting the site triennially (usually in the summer!) to check on their condition. The 36 guns, historically, represent an excellent collection in their own right and the author has not only identified them but shed considerable light on their history through the mysterious marks and engravings appearing on each barrel. Further, he has also provided extremely useful information in Part Two on the innovatory ways in which gunpowder was ignited as well as a very helpful glossary and bibliography.

This is a well-researched and well-written publication which I am sure will appeal both to the enthusiastic schoolchild, the interested adult and the serious researcher.

Philip A. Magrath
Curator of Artillery
Royal Armouries

ACKNOWLEDGEMENTS

In writing this book I have received a great deal of help from many people, all of whom have given most generously of their time and effort. Concerning the castle itself I should like to thank Andrew Whitmarsh, the military history officer of Portsmouth Council, Chrissie Smythe, the senior attendant at the castle, together with Andy Adams and all other members of the castle staff. The curatorial staff at Fort Nelson also provided much advice and help, for which the author gratefully extends his thanks to Nick Hall and in particular Philip McGrath, who cast his eye over the (almost) finished work, commenting on numerous errors committed by the author. Again the staff at the fort have always proved most helpful and their attitude is exemplified by Jim Sadler who (without even having met the author) made and provided the replica friction tube igniter which is illustrated in the chapter headed 'Ignition Systems for Gunpowder'.

In addition to the above, I wish to thank Drs. Ray Riley, Ann Coats and James Thomas, my tutors at Portsmouth University, who first sparked my enthusiasm for the subject of the book, Mr. Peter Webberley, M.A., whose interest and support was appreciated, and Mr. Fred Milbourn M.B.E., for his companionship and transport during the numerous research trips undertaken.

Without doubt, however, my greatest debt of gratitude is due to Mrs. Pauline Milbourn, who typed the text of the book, and whose unfailing patience in response to my numerous textual changes was a source of continued wonder and gratitude on my part. It hardly needs saying that any mistakes in the finished text are entirely the fault of the author.

ABBREVIATIONS USED IN THE TEXT

a.k.a.	Also known as
Arty.	Artillery
av.	Average
B of O	Board of Ordnance
B.L.B.	Blomefield Letter Books
BWIRG	Bulletin of the Wealden Iron Research Group
C in C	Commander in Chief (of the Army)
c.	Circa (approximately)
Capt.	Captain
Cf	Compare with (from Latin confer)
cwt.	Hundredweight (An imperial measure of weight ($1/20^{th}$ of a ton)
DNB	Dictionary of National Biography
e.g.	For example. From the Latin 'exempli gratia'
ESRO	East Sussex Record Office, Pelham House, Lewes
ft.	Foot. An imperial measure of length (often denoted by one tick e.g. 14')
Gen.	General. An Army Officers rank
HMS	His (Her) Majesty's Ship
i.e.	That is to say. From the Latin 'id est' (that is)
Ibid	In the same source (referring to a previously cited work) from Latin 'ibidem'
in(s)	Inch(s) An imperial measurement of length equalling 25.4mms. From the Latin 'uncia' (twelfth part) Often denoted by two ticks after the numeral. E.g. 14"
KIA	Killed in action
lbs.	Pounds avoirdupois. From the Latin 'Libra'
Lt. Gen.	Lieutenant General
MGO	Master General of Ordnance
Mk.	Mark. As in 'Mark 1' Always followed by a numeral. Description of a particular model or type of gun.
MLR	Muzzle loader, rifled. An alternative term for this class of ordnance, used to distinguish between new guns of this type and those converted under Palliser's system which were designated RML.
NCE	New Caxton Encyclopaedia.
oz(s)	Ounce(s) Imperial measurement of weight $1/16^{th}$ of a lb.
p.a.	Per annum
pdr.	Pounder, as in e.g. 9 pounder. This refers to the weight of the shell fired by a gun.
q.v.	Used to direct a reader to another part of a text for further information (from Latin quod vide – 'which see')
R.A.	Royal Artillery.
R.B.F.	Royal Brass Foundry (Woolwich)
R.B.L.	Rifled Breech Loader
R.C.D.	Royal Carriage Department (Woolwich)
R.G.F.	Royal Gun Factory (Woolwich)

ABBREVIATIONS USED IN THE TEXT (CONT'D)

R.M.L.   Rifled Muzzle Loader. A former smooth bored gun which was rifled using the Palliser system.
R.N.   Royal Navy (First used title 'Royal' in reign of Charles II c.1670)
R.N.M.   Royal Naval Museum, Portsmouth
S of S.   Secretary of State
S.B.M.L.   Smooth Bore Muzzle Loader
T.A.   Territorial Army
V & A   Victoria and Albert (Museum)
W.D.   War Department
WIA   Wounded in action
WIRG   Wealden Iron Research Group
yd(s)   Yard(s) An imperial measure of length. 36"(0.9144 metres)

INTRODUCTION

Usually an author writes a book then decides on the cover. This book is possibly the first book ever written to provide a book cover with some content. Some time ago, while taking photographs for what was at that time intended to be my first book, I thought that a photograph of the words 'Southsea Castle' on the castle wall, framed within the breech loop of the gun stationed outside it, would make an ideal book cover. To make this thought a reality, though, would require a book about the castle.

At that time I was intent on writing a (first) book about the recognition features of 18th century ordnance. This intention arose because, when researching the subject for my dissertation at Portsmouth University, it became evident to me that apparently no such comprehensive book existed and all knowledge on the ordnance for the period had to be gained piecemeal. What was required, I thought, was a sort of gun recognition booklet which would enable researchers to identify the origins of a cannon by its appearance, a system for deciphering the various marks on a gun in order to reveal its history.

Such a book would require a great deal of research and would be very time consuming, so it seemed that in the meantime while researching the main book I could quickly produce another (shorter) book of limited subject matter. As I already had the idea for the book cover the 36 guns contained within the castle seemed to provide the perfect limited subject. This present book is the result.

I now know that it is not possible to 'quickly produce' a book which requires research into its subject matter, particularly when the subject ranges beyond the limits of the author's original knowledge. The castle guns are a heterogeneous mix of 18th and 19th century ordnance which includes some foreign guns. Portsmouth Council, the owners of the castle, provided some rudimentary facts about their guns and in some cases little more could be ascertained. Where possible, though, the history of each gun has been investigated. Where areas of doubt exist I have sometimes suggested a provenance but the text will always make clear that my suggestions are only possibilities. In other cases certain historical facts are accepted but as uncertainty is the very nature of history, all I can say is that the book is an honest attempt to provide the facts about the castle guns. Those readers who require a guarantee should buy a toaster.

In anticipation of some minor criticisms I conclude this introduction on a defensive note by pointing out that although the positioning of the guns is as described at the time of writing there may be some small changes over which the author has no control. Also all the photographs taken by the author have the date displayed below. The reason for this is that it is historically useful that the photograph shows the state of the gun at the date of writing, revealing marks etc. on the gun which may eventually become lost through the passage of time.

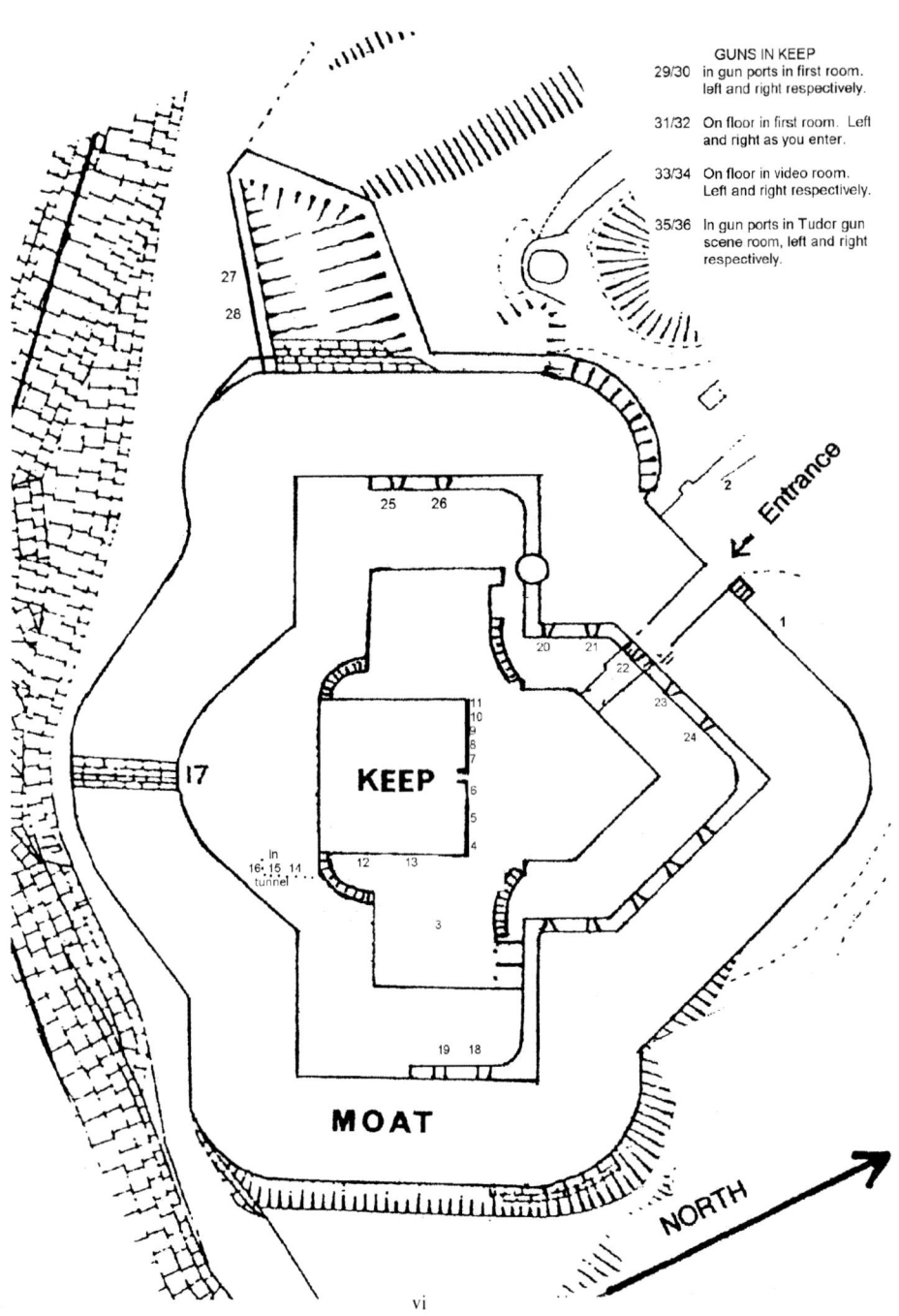

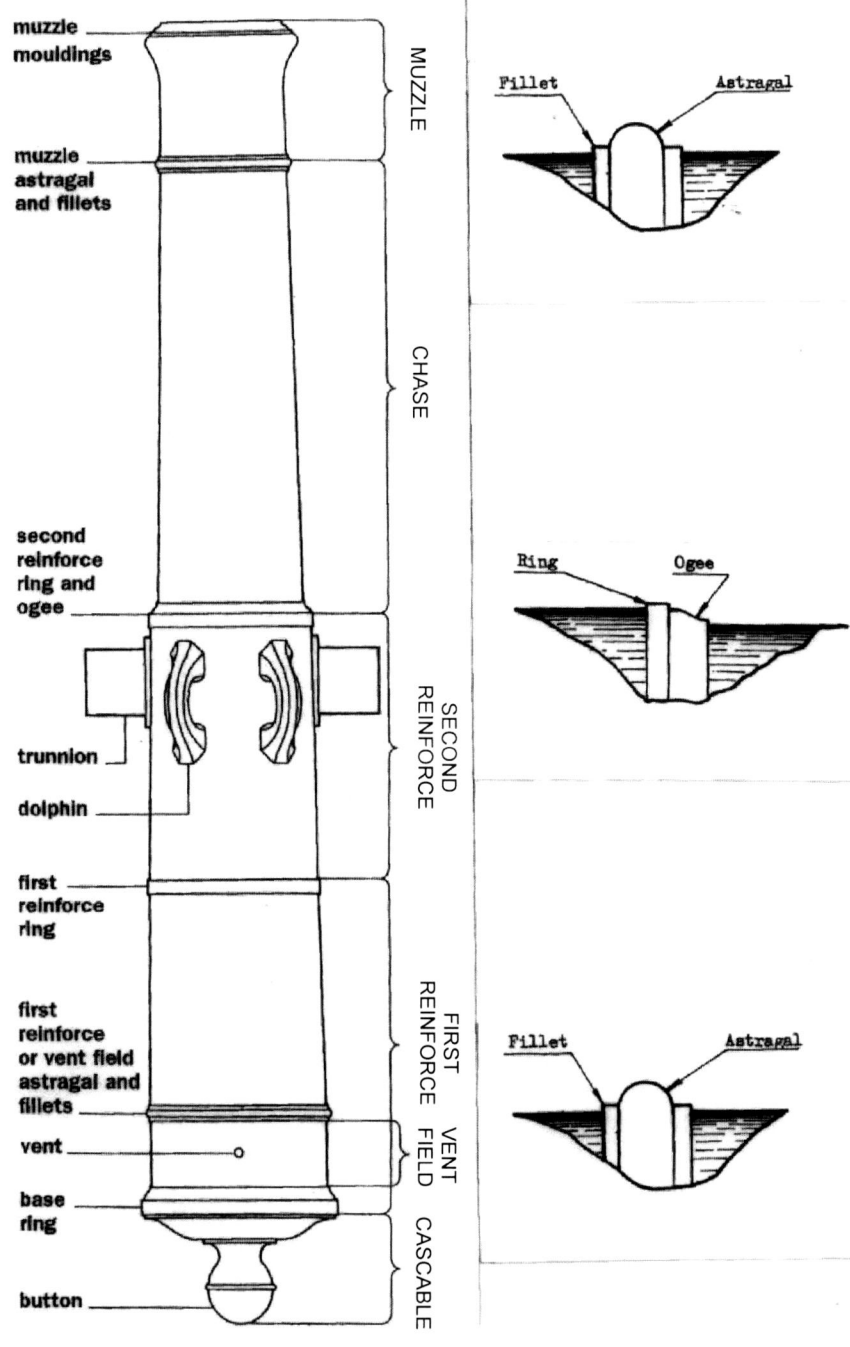

PART 1

image © A.L. Boxell (10.04.2007)

Entrance to the castle is gained by a gateway through the north bastion after crossing the dry moat. In passing, the coat of arms of Charles II above the gateway is worth examination.

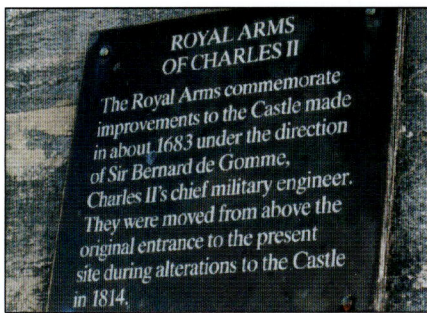 

image © A.L. Boxell (10.04.2007)   image © A.L. Boxell (10.04.2007)

An explanatory plaque to the left of the gateway provides information about this impressive example of stone masonry. Through the gateway guns numbers 4 and 5 can already be seen, while the Royal Arms are overlooked by a Victorian cannon (gun No. 22. on plan).

Before crossing the moat the visitor will already have passed two guns (numbered 1 & 2 on the plan) flanking the entrance to the castle, whose descriptions can be found in the appropriate section of the book. In examining the castle's guns the visitor may select his own route, checking the location of each gun by reference to the plan enclosed. Although correct at time of printing these locations may change slightly due to the on-going conservation work at the castle, but reference to the photographs and descriptions of the guns should clarify any confusion which may result.

SOUTHSEA CASTLE
Gun. No. 1

A veteran of the Crimea

image © A.L. Boxell (31.10.2008)

image © A.L. Boxell (31.10.2008)

PHOTOGRAPHS AND DESCRIPTIONS OF GUNS

Each description is preceded by information identifying the gun as follows:-

The gun number in the first column refers to a number on the enclosed plan of the castle. In some cases (usually guns on loan from other museums) the museum number is also shown. The 'accession' number in the second column is Portsmouth Council's reference for the gun, showing the year of acquisition and the Council's identifying number, while the location of the gun is shown in the third column.

In the description following the identifying information the various markings on the gun refer to markings recorded as being on the gun in the past (which may no longer be visible owing to the ravages of time) and marks uncovered more recently.

GUN NO. 1 As shown on map of castle (Mus. No. H6917)	ACCESSION NO. GUN TYPE/ CARRIAGE 1969/290 British 68pdr. (8") SBML on Garrison standing carriage	LOCATION Outside castle, to left of gateway as you approach the castle

MEASUREMENTS

BARREL length	CASCABLE dia.	TRUNNION dia.	BORE dia.
10'	28"	8"	8"

INFORMATION
This gun, purchased by Portsmouth Council in 1969 from Parnell, Daniel and Morrell of Honiton in Devon, is an example of the heaviest smooth bore muzzle loader (SBML) gun used in the British service. Designed by Dundas, it is mounted on a wrought iron carriage intended for a Howitzer. A nearby plaque provides some information about the gun and suggests that the piece was engaged in the siege of Sevastopol (Oct. 1854-Sept 1855).

MARKS ON GUN
The foundry mark 'W Co', which can be seen on the left trunnion, shows that the gun was made by the Walker Company. This company, founded in 1746 by Samuel Walker, was chosen by Thomas Blomefield, the Inspector of Artillery, to develop the Blomefield pattern gun which he devised in 1787. Based at Rotherham the original Walker Co. was wound up in 1817 but in 1820 a grandson of the original firm's founder, also called Samuel, took over the Gospel Oak ironworks at Tipton, Staffs, using the same foundry mark as his grandfather until the firm finally closed down circa 1860.

The date 1853 above the first reinforce shows therefore that the gun was cast in that year at Tipton

SOUTHSEA CASTLE

Gun No. 1

Raised vent patch drilled to accept flintlock igniter

image © A.L. Boxell (06.09.2008)

Right side of gun. Detail of 'skeleton' type carriage

image © A.L. Boxell (06.09.2008)

On the first reinforce the government broad arrow mark indicates that the gun was accepted for service use after being 'proved' by undergoing a series of tests culminating in the firing of a succession of heavy loads. This crowsfoot mark, as it was sometimes called, was actually employed to mark all government property, but as no gun would be accepted into government service without being proved the mark doubled as a proof mark for ordnance.

Also on the first reinforce the weight of the gun (96-0-0) is shown in hundredweights, quarters and pounds (cwts./qrs./lbs.)

The mark 36 on the right trunnion is possibly a foundry mark indicating a batch number.

The gun exhibits all the main features of the Blomefield pattern, although the breeching loop which Blomefield placed above the button has been lowered in order to pierce the button, bringing it to a position in the centre line of the gun. This adaptation of the original design, attributed to Congreve, was, with the addition of a gate, "subsequently adopted in all designs of gun" (Caruana II p. 318). Examples of this adaptation can be found in several guns within the castle (e.g. guns, 20,21 and 22) while guns 18 and 19 are examples of the original Blomefield pattern, having the breeching loop above the button.

Other features of Blomefield's design can be seen in the general lack of ornamentation, the vent patch drilled for the attachment of the flintlock firing mechanism and the smooth curve of the cascable so that it describes a single curve of uniform thickness whose centre is located in the chamber where the powder explodes. (see photo.) This design eliminated several obvious sources of weakness found on the type of cascable adorned with rings and reverse curves which can be seen on other guns within the castle.

image © A.L. Boxell (30.08.2006)

[1] "A gate is a removable arc inserted in the circle of the breeching loop, which can be slid out to remove the breeching" (Caruana II p. 318) It is held in place by a pin.

SOUTHSEA CASTLE

Gun No. 1
Foundry logo (Walker Co.) shown on left trunnion

image © A.L. Boxell (13.09.2008)

Right trunnion. Different sized plates can be bolted into the trunnion holes so that they can accept various other calibres of gun. The lines are used when levelling the weapon

image © A.L. Boxell (13.09.2008)

CARRIAGE

Standing carriages of this type were constructed of wrought iron. They were proposed by Col. Clerk R.A. and approved on 2nd September 1867. (Le Mesurier p.54) These carriages were quite versatile and could be used to mount different types of gun by inserting various plates and collars into the trunnion hole. Additionally by removing the rear trucks (wheels) the carriage could be used as a rear chock type.

In the view of the gun below, seen along the barrel from the rear, the crowsfoot mark can still be seen on the first reinforce but the date and weight of the gun mentioned in the text are now virtually indecipherable.

image © A.L. Boxell (31.08.2008)

SOUTHSEA CASTLE

Gun No. 2
Guarding the entrance to the Castle

image © A.L. Boxell (10.04.2007)

image © A.L. Boxell (10.04.2007)

GUN NO. 2 On plan Other No. H6972	ACCESSION No./ GUN TYPE/CARRIAGE 1969/431 British MKIII Armstrong-Fraser 9" 12ton. RML	LOCATION Outside castle, to right of gateway as you approach it.

MEASUREMENTS

BARREL Length 145(121)	CASCABLE dia. 38	TRUNNION dia. 12	BORE dia. 9

INFORMATION

This gun, a rifled muzzle loader, was an adaptation of a new pattern of wrought iron gun originally designed by Sir William George Armstrong in 1856. The original Armstrong gun was a rifled *breech* loader (R.B.L) of revolutionary design in that the inner tube of the barrel was surrounded by coiled wire which was then covered by wrought iron. While the rifling increased accuracy the concomitant lack of windage (cf) increased the breech pressure, so several jackets were shrunk on to the breech end to compensate for this increase.

The Fraser modification consisted of the "use of a few large hoops (instead of several small ones) by forming two thick coils, one upon the other, without *separate* welding or machining. The mass thus formed was welded together, but the advantage of the separate shrinkage of the coils was of course lost". (Lloyd and Hadcock p.40) This modification departed from Armstrong's theory but, as it was more economical, it was used at Woolwich until steel superseded wrought iron.

In 1863 the government ceased ordering artillery from Armstrong and for a number of years reverted to muzzle loaders, of which this gun manufactured in 1868 is an example.

Several reasons have been assumed for this reversion, the most likely centring around failures of the Armstrong breech mechanism. It is, however, generally agreed that Armstrong's gun designs marked the birth of modern artillery.

There is some ambiguity on the plaque describing this gun, which states that "guns of this type [i.e. *muzzle* loaders] formed the major part of the heavy armament of the 1860... (Palmerston) defences." As explained above from 1856 to 1863 the Armstrong pattern guns were *breech* loaders. It is of course possible that the Royal Commission of 1860 recommended the reversion to muzzle loaders and that this recommendation was not implemented until 1863.

MARKS ON GUN

No marks are now apparent although the gun was formerly marked RGF 1868 on left trunnion. This would indicate that the gun was manufactured at the Royal Gun Factory at Woolwich in 1868

SOUTHSEA CASTLE

Gun No. 3

image © A.L. Boxell (26.04.2007)

Mk 1 9pdr.RML of 8cwt. Mounted on the Mk.1 Naval carriage

image © A.L. Boxell (26.04.2007)

GUN NO. 3 As shown on plan	ACCESSION No./ GUN TYPE/CARRIAGE 1970/546 British 9pdr. Steel gun of Armstrong pattern on 1880 carriage	LOCATION In courtyard to left of the keep as you enter the castle

MEASUREMENTS

BARREL Length 5'7"	CASCABLE dia. 9"	TRUNNION dia. 3½"	BORE dia. 3"

INFORMATION

No provenance is available. Judging by the barrel length this gun appears to be the MarkI pattern, 9pdr. RML of 8cwt. According to Lloyd and Hadcock (p.268) this pattern was designed in 1866 but was not adopted until 1870. The long delay between design and introduction into service is accounted for by the fact that the guns underwent 'a great number of trials' (*ibid*).

The mark II 9pdr. of 6cwt., differed in that it had a barrel some 3" longer (Blackmore p. 92) and was designed in 1874 for use by the Royal Horse Artillery. It differed also in having a swell at the muzzle and a dispart patch with protective shoulders for the fore sight.

In 1879 some mark II 6cwt. guns were adopted for sea service, becoming known as the Mark IV. They were mounted on the Mark I Naval Travelling Carriage, designed for naval use ashore.[2]

Gun No. 3 at Southsea Castle, then, is a Mk.I 9pdr. RML of 8cwt. *land* service gun, mounted on the Mk.I *Naval* carriage. The steel barrel of this Mk.I has three groove rifling and is surrounded at the breech end by a jacket encasing the coiled wire which supported the barrel in Armstrong's design. These jackets were originally of wrought iron but on this gun the jacket is made of steel. The muzzle is surmounted by a small block, drilled and threaded and protected by a preserving screw. The cascable is slotted centrally and it seems evident that this slot would have contained a rear sight which could be aligned with a (removable) fore sight screwed to the aforementioned block at the muzzle. This gun, unlike the Mk II, does not have a swell at the muzzle, presumably because this would have complicated the fore sight arrangement.

The trunnions are of larger diameter than the bore and are supported by shoulders. They seem to be placed rather higher than is normal, bringing them nearer to the horizontal axis of the bore. This feature may have been intended to ameliorate the excessive jump (see glossary) which Lloyd and Hadcock (p. 269) attribute to these guns being mounted on short trail carriages.

---

[2] Further information on carriages is provided in the appropriate section.

SOUTHSEA CASTLE

Gun No. 3
Guns Nos. 12 and 13 can be seen in the background

image © A.L. Boxell (26.04.2007)

Lower picture, showing how elevating gear is fitted to naval carriage, was taken at Fort Nelson. Shown here by kind permission of the Board of Trustees of the Royal Armouries.

MARKS ON GUN

At the breech end the monogram of Queen Victoria is incised on the jacket. It is clear that this gun is identical to gun number 25 on the west platform and the two guns may have been part of the same battery as they are marked 82 and 83, respectively, on the breech. These numbers were probably added at battery level after the gun came into service, as the foundry would have marked the gun number on the left trunnion.[3] Unfortunately RGF marks on gun 3 are not apparent but it seems likely that the gun would have been manufactured there some time after 1866 when this pattern of gun was designed.

CARRIAGE

A plaque on the carriage provides information from which it is apparent that it is an 1880 design intended to carry a 9 pounder Rifled Muzzle Loader (RML) gun weighing either 8 or 6 hundredweight (cwt). The letters W.D. flanking the government broad arrow stand for War Department and RCD means Royal Carriage Department. The figure I which precedes the letters RCD probably indicates that the carriage is the Mark one Naval Travelling Carriage previously mentioned.

Below the date (1880) the information provided is even more esoteric but is reproduced here in order to conserve it. REG No. 46W CARR. 448 WHEELS 291. Reg. No. probably means registered or registration number (of the type of carriage?) Carr. Would be carriage 448 (the number of this particular carriage?) and wheels 291 might designate the type of wheels for this size carriage as several sizes of wheels were in service at the same time. The wheels actually fitted here are of 42" (3'6") diameter, but larger wheels were in service for RML guns mounted on different types of carriage.[4]

Information held by the Council shows that the 42" wheel was formerly marked RCD T 6235 and the date 1880 appeared on the wheel hub. These marks no longer exist. The wheel is shod with a metal ring tyre,[5] but the bolts are missing.

The elevating gear, which was operated by a hand wheel at the rear of the gearbox, is also missing, although two 'omega' shaped supports bolted to the trail brackets are obviously intended to secure the gear mechanism. These supports are incorrect, being of a type which would not restrict the lateral movement of the mechanism. The correct type of support has closed ends and appears to be made of bronze. (see photos.). Other supports on the trail brackets are intended to secure the handspike and sponge and a metal socket is provided to hold the priming irons or prickers. (Blackmore p. 93)

---

[3]. The RGF provided the following information on the left trunnion of 9pdrs. RGF., Gun No., Mark No., and Year of Manufacture. Some of these marks are still legible on gun 25 from which it can be seen that the gun no. was 106? The numbers 82 and 83 on the breech, then, would probably have been added at unit level to simplify identification, rather like the 'butt numbers' painted on rifles in unit armouries.

[4] The Mk I *Naval* carriage of 1885 should not be confused with the MK 1 carriage for *land* service, which was larger and came equipped with axletree boxes which also served as seats for two members of the gun crew. Both the Mk. I land service and the Mk. II *land* service (which was even larger and carried the 16pdr. RML) can be quickly identified by these axletree boxes and the fact that the wheel for the elevating gear is located on the right side, rather than centrally.

[5]. There were two types of metal tyre in service; the ring (or hoop) tyre and the streak (or strake) tyre. For information about these see glossary.

These photographs were taken at Fort Nelson in order to show how the elevating gear was fitted to the naval carriage. They are shown by kind permission of the Board of Trustees of the Royal Armouries

AUTHOR'S NOTE
The information provided with respect to gun No. 3 is the result of painstaking research involving much travel and background reading. Despite this it is possible that some facts are incorrect for which I apologise in advance. The difficulties encountered may be better understood if it is realised that there were five types of 9pdr. RML guns and at least three types of carriage, which is why these pieces are universally known as the 'nine pounder nightmares' (or would be if I had anything to do with it!).

image © A.L. Boxell (26.04.2007)

SOUTHSEA CASTLE

Gun No. 4

image © A.L. Boxell (05.04.2007)

A Georgian 3pdr. cast in 1814

image © A.L. Boxell (09.05.2007)

Elevating gear. Note quarter sight marks on base ring.

GUN NO. 4	ACCESSION NO./GUN TYPE/ CARRIAGE	LOCATION North Bailey
As shown on plan	1970/399 British 3pdr. Brass field gun on reconstructed (Congreve block trail) carriage	Left of keep entrance – left hand gun

MEASUREMENTS

BARREL length 3'11"	CASCABLE dia. 7½"	TRUNNION dia. 2¼"	BORE dia 3"

INFORMATION

Purchased by Portsmouth Council from Weller and Dufty Ltd., of 141 Bromsgrove Street Birmingham, this 3pdr. brass field gun was cast in 1814 at the Royal Brass Foundry Woolwich. The block trail carriage was designed to resist the force of recoil to some extent thereby reducing time spent in reloading. A hook underneath the carriage provided a convenient point to hang the water bucket, enabling the gun crew to wet the sponge used to swab out the barrel between shots. This procedure, a necessary part of the reloading drill, was designed to prevent premature ignition of the next cartridge by glowing particles left in the barrel after firing. It is interesting to compare the wheel flanges of this carriage with those of the Victorian 9pdr. (gun No. 3). Whereas the wheels of the heavier gun have been provided with a lynchpin to make them more easily removable their design makes them more likely to snag when used in thick undergrowth. In the lighter gun the smooth wheel hub obviates this tendency, but at the expense of some loss of speed in replacing a wheel should it become necessary

The gun is equipped with elevating gear, together with a central sight notch on the muzzle and on the cascable band. The raised vent rib has not been drilled for the attachment of a flintlock firing mechanism as the artillery (unlike the R.N.) did not adopt the flintlock for general issue until the 1830s. (Wilkinson-Latham p. 40)

MARKS ON GUN

In addition to the sight notches mentioned above quarter sight markings can be seen on the cascable. On the first reinforce band the name of the gun founder and the casting date are shown. The man named thereon, Henry King, was the first native of these shores to hold the post of Master Founder of the Royal Brass Foundry (see history of R.B.F). On the second reinforce band the roman numerals DVII (507) represent the production number of the piece.[6] On the first reinforce the Royal cipher of George III can be identified and on the

---

[6] It seems evident from information held in the catalogue of the Tower Armouries that these 3pdrs. were numbered consecutively, as they were produced, in the RBF at Woolwich. A similar gun proved on 27th October 1813 is numbered ccccxci (491) and further back still, in 1807, another gun of identical type bears the number cxcv (195).
Three similar guns cast at Woolwich in 1801 (rather more ornamental so probably made as gifts for a foreign ruler) have the foundry numbers 140,143 and 145. (Blackmore pp. 83 – 85)

SOUTHSEA CASTLE

Gun No. 4.

The Royal cipher of George III can clearly be seen on the first reinforce. Just ahead of it the name of the founder and the date of casting are shown on the reinforce band.

image ©A.L. Boxell (10.07.2007)

chase the cipher of the Earl of Mulgrave, who held the post of Master General of the Ordnance from 1810 to 1818.

Although Henry Earl of Mulgrave (family name Phipps) had seen action in the American War of Independence and had also been stationed in the Caribbean his main impact on public life was as a diplomat and politician. Prior to his appointment as MGO he had been Foreign Secretary (1805) and First Lord of the Admiralty, but found the demands of the latter post too burdensome. Consequently he was transferred to the cabinet post of MGO in 1810, eventually relinquishing it to the Duke of Wellington in 1818. Mulgrave's tenure of the post was unremarkable and it is apparent from a contemporary account (Joseph Farington 1-3-1820) that Mulgrave's health was failing and by 1820 he would have been unable to carry out his duties even had he wished to do so. (Details extracted from DNB "Phipps" pp.184-186).

Cipher of the Earl of Mulgrave, Master General of the Ordnance,
1810 - 1818

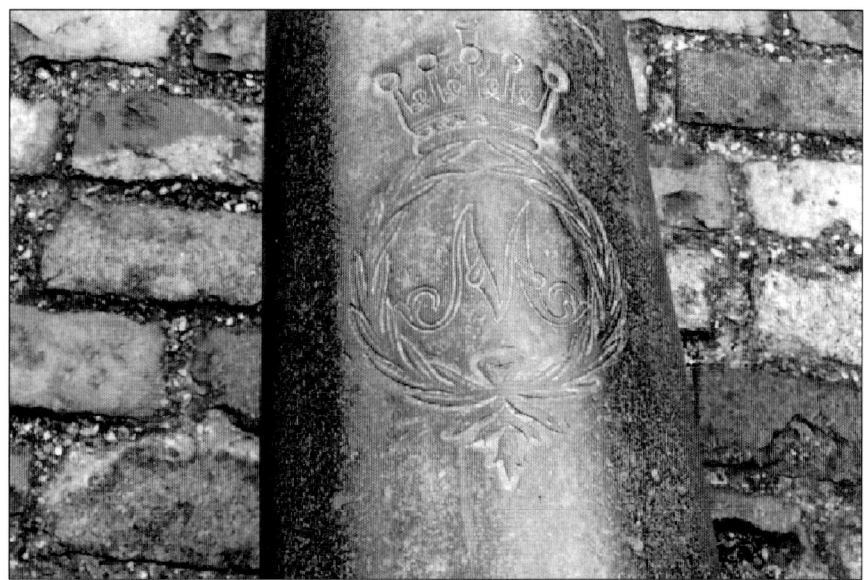

image ©A.L. Boxell (10.07.2007)

SOUTHSEA CASTLE

Gun No. 4
Serial No. of gun in roman numerals.

image ©A.L. Boxell (10.07.2007)

Elevating gear attached to button.

image ©A.L. Boxell (11.05.2007)

SOUTHSEA CASTLE

Gun No. 4

Compare the smooth wheel hubs of this Georgian gun with
the pinned design of the Victorian gun shown below it.

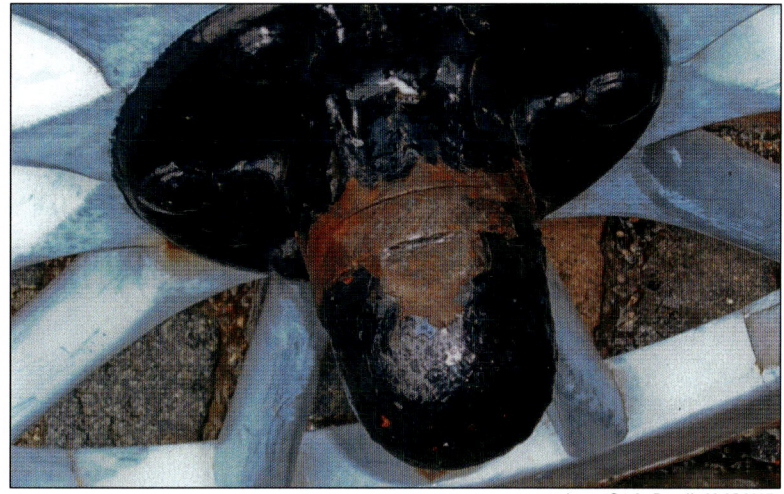

image ©A.L. Boxell (09.05.2007)

Wheels of guns 3 and 25 held by lynch pins

image ©A.L. Boxell (09.05.2007)

SOUTHSEA CASTLE

Gun No. 5

DOLPHINS
These were the handles used for lifting the gun. (Visitors are requested not to try)
Both photos are shown by kind permission of the Board of Trustees of Royal Armouries.

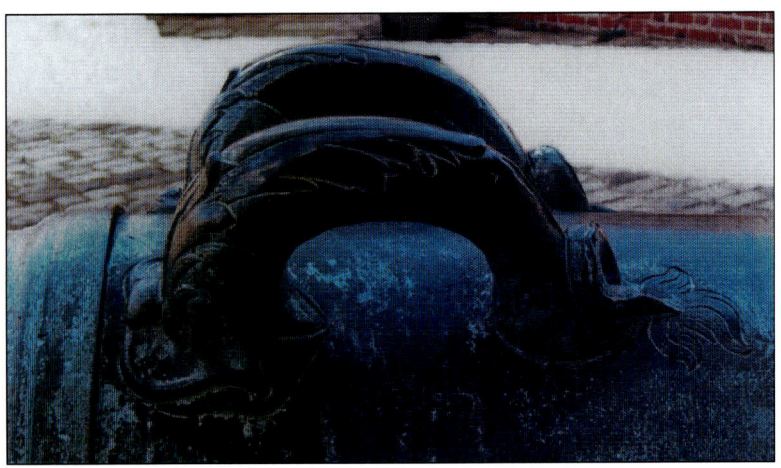

GUN NO. 5 on plan	ACCESSION NO. GUN TYPE/ CARRIAGE	LOCATION
	On loan from Royal Armouries (XIX. 48)	North Bailey In line with main entrance
	British 24pdr. Brass muzzle loader (see *Gun Metals. Brass, Bronze and Iron*')	

MEASUREMENTS

BARREL length 9' 4¾"	CASCABLE dia. 20"	TRUNNION dia. 5 $7/_8$"	BORE dia. 6"

INFORMATION

The 'Royal George' gun, as it is known, has had a colourful history. A 24pdr. naval gun, on loan from Royal Armouries, Tower of London, it is mounted on a naval truck carriage and despite its age is in fine condition. A plaque on the carriage gives brief details of the gun's history and it is apparent that it was in service for nearly forty years before going down with the *Royal George*, a first rate which foundered in 1782[7] Another plaque affixed to the chase of the gun provides information about its eventual recovery from the wreck. As the curvature of the barrel makes this plaque somewhat difficult to read it is reproduced below.

"THIS GUN, WHICH FORMED PART OF THE ARMAMENT OF THE ROYAL GEORGE, WAS RECOVERED FROM THE WRECK OF THAT SHIP BY M[R] CHA[S] ANT[Y] DEAN IN THE YEAR 1834"

At the breech end of the gun the vent patch is raised above the vent field but it has not been horizontally drilled for the attachment of a flintlock as the gun pre-dates Anson's order of 21st Oct. 1755 (ADM 2/225) authorising the issue of these gun locks. The gun is furnished with 'dolphins'. These were essentially handles used for hoisting the barrel but as they were almost always made in the form of dolphins the name became synonymous with these handles whether they were cast in that form or not.

---

[7] For readers unfamiliar with the rating system (formerly) employed to differentiate between various types of ships of the line a 'first rate' was a ship equipped with a hundred guns, or more. (see footnote to gun No.11 for a fuller explanation of the rating system) One such ship, the *Royal George*, sank at her moorings in calm weather after some of her guns were moved to heel the ship over in order to enable an outside water cock to be replaced. The court martial investigating the circumstances of her loss seemed determined to believe that heeling the ship caused undue strain on rotten timbers and the bottom of the ship simply dropped out. An alternative eye witness account by crew member James Ingram suggests that heeling the ship caused an influx of water through the lower gun ports (document held at Nat. Maritime Mus.) Subsequently, it is alleged, the R.N. resisted all attempts to salvage the wreck to establish the facts. Many of her guns, however, were salvaged and melted down, the metals so obtained eventually being used to form part of Nelson's Column.

SOUTHSEA CASTLE

Gun No. 5
The weight of the gun on the cascable can be seen just below the maker's name and date of the casting and just ahead of these the raised vent patch mentioned in the text.

Both photos are shown by kind permission of the Board of Trustees of Royal Armouries

MARKS ON THE GUN
On the Cascable the weight of the piece is shown as 51cwt. 1qtr. 0lbs. (51-1-0) just above these figures the name of the gun maker (A. Schalch) together with the casting date (1743) is shown on the base ring. [8]

Moving forward past the vent field the coat of arms of George II stands in relief on the first reinforce. On brass guns such as this, full coats of arms were often depicted, whereas on iron guns it is more usual to find only the ciphers of the reigning monarch and his Master General of Ordnance. Ahead of the dolphins on the chase the coat of arms of John, second Duke of Montague (Master Gen. of Ordnance 1740 to 1749 with a brief interruption in 1742) is also shown in relief.

Photo below is shown by kind permission of the Board of Trustees of Royal Armouries.

[8] 'A. SCHALCH FECIT 1743.' The Latin word 'Fecit' comes from the verb Facere meaning 'to make' in that language. Andreas Schalch, a Swiss National, was the first Master Founder of the R.B.F. This government-run foundry was set up at Woolwich in 1717 by the Board of Ordnance. Schalch worked at Woolwich for 54 years before (reluctantly) relinquishing his post to two Dutchmen, the Verbruggens,

SOUTHSEA CASTLE

Gun No. 5
Coat of Arms of John, 2nd Duke of Montague

This photo shown by kind permission of the Board of Trustees of Royal Armouries

John Montague, (1690-1749) was reputed to be a kindhearted and benevolent man but was said to be 'puckish and eccentric from birth'. (DNB). His sense of humour and love of practical jokes meant that he was considered to be rather frivolous although he held many responsible positions, rising to the rank of General in the Army. Despite this his military career was inauspicious. At age sixteen he volunteered for Flanders but finding that he had 'little taste for war's carnage', (DNB) he soon returned home. He seems to have made little impact as Master General of the Ordnance (1740 – 1749)

SOUTHSEA CASTLE
Gun No. 6

image ©A.L. Boxell (05.04.2007)

image ©A.L. Boxell (05.04.2007)

SOUTHSEA CASTLE

Gun No. 6

The monogram of Charles III of Spain (1716-1788) King of Spain from 1759, he conducted two wars against Britain during his reign, in the second of which the Spanish unsuccessfully laid siege to Gibraltar for a number of years.

image ©A.L. Boxell (05.04.2007)

GUN NO. 6 on plan	ACCESSION NO. /GUN TYPE/ CARRIAGE 1968/300 Spanish Brass 6pdr. SBML. Mounted on rear chock carriage	LOCATION Immediately to left of keep entrance

MEASUREMENTS

BARREL length 5'1½"	CASCABLE dia. 9½"	TRUNNION dia. 3¼"	BORE dia. 3⅝"

INFORMATION
This Spanish gun, one of four, was purchased from a dealer, Charles Perry, with the help of a grant from the Victoria and Albert museum. A naval gun, it formed part of the armament of a privateer, the *Louisa*, which was owned by the Craven family.

Although the gun is mounted on a rear chock carriage this may not be its original mounting. At 3.66 the calibre is unusual, although this might be more usual when expressed in centimetres (9.5cms). The diameter of the trunnions (3¼") is rather less than the bore size and this too might be considered unusual by English cannon makers, who tended to make these two diameters the same.

MARKS ON GUN.
On the base ring the marks showing the place and date of casting (Seville 30th April 1777) are quite clear, despite being written in Spanish and indicate that the royal arms incised on the first reinforce must be those of Charles III of Spain. The marks on the trunnions are equally clear but divulge rather less information. The left trunnion, for example, has a mark reminiscent of a shorthand symbol plus three figures or letters which could be 555 or SSS. On the right trunnion the mark P° 770# is the weight of the gun, while 'FIERA', on the chase, is the name of the gun.

image ©A.L. Boxell (08.05.2008)

SOUTHSEA CASTLE

Gun No. 6
Mark on base ring – "Sevilla 30 de Abril de 1777"

image ©A.L. Boxell (01.09.2008)

Gun 6 in foreground with guns 7-11 in background

image ©A.L. Boxell (01.09.2008)

In the North Bailey, just to the right of the entrance to the Keep, lie several un-mounted barrels. The first of these is painted black and is not included in the castle's numbering system as it belongs to the Cumberland Guard, a re-enactment group based at the castle. A 9pdr. rifled muzzle loader, it has no visible marks except a very indistinct royal cipher which appears to be that of Queen Victoria.

To the right of the Guard's cannon in a line, a further five barrels (numbered 7 to 11) present a rather sorry appearance. They are all very worn and identification is difficult. Although they are all reputedly howitzers this description has been challenged.

image ©A.L. Boxell (11.06.2007)

GUN NO. 7 on plan	ACCESSION NO./GUN TYPE/ CARRIAGE 1970/542 British 12pdr. Brass SBML, no carriage.	LOCATION North Bailey in line of barrels to right of Keep entrance

MEASUREMENTS

BARREL Length 45"	CASCABLE dia. 10"	TRUNNION dia. 3½"	BORE dia. 4½"

INFORMATION
Gun number 7, the first barrel in the line to the right of the black Cumberland Guard gun, is a Victorian gun of the Millar pattern.[9] It weighs 6½cwt. and the calibre is 4" (11.6cms). The gun, which has a rudimentary foresight incorporated in the muzzle and appears to have provision for a rear sight, was purchased from the Director of Naval Armaments Supply at Bath and was initially kept at Priddy's Hard.

---

[9]. Lieut. Gen. William Millar was Inspector General of Woolwich 1827-38

SOUTHSEA CASTLE

Gun No. 7

Marks on the gun, moving up the barrel from the breech end. Just in front of the vent (lower picture) the cipher of Queen Victoria can be seen, with the weight of the gun just in front. The serial number of the gun is shown between the trunnions (upper picture)

image ©A.L. Boxell (16.08.2008)

image ©A.L. Boxell (15.09.2008)

MARKS ON GUN

On the base ring the casting date (1855) and the name 'Eccles' can be seen. Samuel Eccles was the foreman of the Royal Brass Foundry at Woolwich Arsenal and this is one of several existing guns which bear his name. On the first reinforce the distinctive shape of Queen Victoria's cipher can be made out. (one of three used by that monarch at various times) Further along the barrel, on the chase, the cipher of Lord Raglan can still be discerned, although it is very worn.

Traditionally it had always been normal practice for a cannon to have both the royal cipher and that of the current Master General of Ordnance (M.G.O.) represented on the barrel. In 1852 Lord Raglan was appointed MGO. However, in 1854 Raglan, while still holding the post of MGO, was posted to the Crimea to take command of British forces there. In 1855 the newly appointed Secretary of State for War (S of S), Lord Panmure, taking advantage of the incumbent's absence in the Crimea, abolished the post of MGO by an order in council dated 6th June 1855, (DNB p.427 'Maule') dividing its former responsibilities between the Commander in Chief of the Army (C in C) and the S of S for War. Faced with a *fait accompli* Raglan's belated protests were in vain, and were in any case literally short-lived as he died in the Crimea on 28th June 1855. The post of MGO died with him

image ©A.L. Boxell (10.07.2007)

SOUTHSEA CASTLE

Gun No. 7

On the chase, near the muzzle, the cipher of Lord Raglan dates the gun between 1852 when he became Master General of Ordnance and 1855, when that post was abolished. Raglan's name will always be associated with the ill-fated charge of the Light Brigade, when a misunderstood order from Raglan caused the famous cavalry charge at Balaclava. On the cipher the motto '*Tria Juncta in Uno*' can just be discerned surrounding the letter *R*, the whole surmounted by the baronial coronet.

image ©A.L. Boxell (15.09.2008)

GUN NO. 8 on plan	ACCESSION NO./GUN TYPE/ CARRIAGE Accession no. uncertain. British 12pdr. SBML (Millar pattern) No carriage.	LOCATION North Bailey. Right of Keep entrance.

MEASUREMENTS

BARREL Length 45"	CASCABLE dia. 10"	TRUNNION dia. 3½"	BORE dia. 4½"

INFORMATION

Very little information is available from Council records about this gun, and, additionally, the gun is so worn that little information can be gleaned from observation. It has been described as a howitzer and is apparently identical to the two which flank it. In common with the other Millar pattern guns in this line it has a dispart patch on the muzzle which serves as a rudimentary foresight.

MARKS ON GUN

However, the gun can be dated very accurately by reference to the MGO's cipher on the chase. Despite the fact that this cipher is only discernible in outline the similarity of shape between it and the cipher on gun No. 9 alongside is evident. Fortunately gun 9 bears the confirmatory date 1849 on its base ring, which identifies the cipher as that of the Marquis of Anglesey, who occupied the post of MGO twice (1827-8 and 1846-52) In similar fashion the outline of the royal cipher of Queen Victoria can be identified, again by comparison of its shape with those of the guns on either side. As Victoria did not come to the throne until 1837 Anglesey's cipher obviously refers to his second term of office. Gun No. 8, therefore, was cast between 1846 and 1852.

Henry William Paget, the Marquis of Anglesey, was a brilliant cavalry commander who made a fine reputation during the Peninsular War. He again distinguished himself at Waterloo, where he had 'eight or nine horses shot under him' (DNB p.357) before himself losing his right leg to enemy grapeshot. Later the first articulated artificial limb ever devised, the 'Anglesey leg' was fitted to his stump.

In 1827 Anglesey succeeded Wellington as MGO but only remained in post until 1828. In 1846 he was again MGO until 1852, at which time he was nearly eighty-four. During his second term in that office he continually stressed the need for coastal defence against the new threat to the Empire posed by steamships

SOUTHSEA CASTLE

First Marquess of Anglesey, Master General of Ordnance 1827/8 & 1846-52

Henry William Paget (1768 – 1854)
By
Sir Thomas Lawrence.
Circa 1816

GUN NO. 9	ACCESSION No./GUN TYPE/CARRIAGE Accession No. uncertain. British 12pdr. SBML Millar pattern gun. No carriage.	LOCATION North Bailey. Right of Keep entrance.

MEASUREMENTS

BARREL Length 45"	CASCABLE dia. 10"	TRUNNION dia. 3½"	BORE dia. 4½"

INFORMATION
From its similarity in size and shape to the two preceding guns, this gun is likely also to be of their type. Apart from this little information is available.

MARKS ON GUN
On the base ring the casting date, 1849, is clearly visible. Unfortunately the letters accompanying the date are badly worn and interpretation is not helped by the cramped location of the piece. It has been suggested that the words preceding the date are 'Low Moor'. This reading seemed improbable as after 1774 the Royal Brass Foundry (RBF) supplied all requirements for brass cannon and Schalch's previous system of contracting out some of this type of work ended.[10] (Jackson and De Beer p.49) It is unlikely, too, that the Low Moor Iron Co., would have diversified their cannon production, even had government contracts for brass guns been available in 1849 when this cannon was made. Normal practice for brass cannon was to show the Founder's name and date on the base ring, and bearing this in mind it was eventually ascertained that the name 'W. North' preceded the date on this cannon.[11] This was the name of the assistant founder at that time. It therefore seems certain that this gun was cast at the RBF in 1849, the work being supervised by Mr. North. (See *Royal Brass Foundry*).

Moving up the barrel the Royal cipher of Queen Victoria is evident but the figures showing the weight of the piece on the first reinforce band are too worn to provide any useful information. On the second reinforce band the number 112 in roman numerals (CXII) is probably the production number of the gun. On the chase the cipher of Henry, Marquis of Anglesey (MGO 1827/8 and 1846-52) can be identified.

---

[10] The Royal Brass Foundry was set up in 1717 following an accident at the Moorfields Foundry of Mathew Bagley, which convinced the government that they needed a foundry under their control. The first Master Founder was Andrew Schalch, a Swiss national. He was replaced in 1772 by two Dutchmen, the Verbruggens, who modernised the foundry by introducing new techniques.
[11] The engraved writing on the base ring of the cannon was chalked over. After the surplus chalk had been removed from the surface, the chalk which remained in the incisions gave a clear picture of the writing (see photo)

SOUTHSEA CASTLE

Gun No. 9
Monogram of Henry, Marquis of Anglesey is shown on the chase.
He was Master General of Ordnance 1827-8 and 1846-52.

image ©A.L. Boxell (15.09.2008)

Name of Assistant Founder, Royal Brass Factory on base ring.
Date on which gun was cast, 1849, is also shown.

image ©A.L. Boxell (12.06.2007)

GUN NO. 10 on plan	ACCESSION No./GUN TYPE/ CARRIAGE Accession no. uncertain. British 24pdr. SBML brass gun. No carriage	LOCATION North Bailey to the right of Keep entrance

MEASUREMENTS

BARREL Length 57" (4'9")	CASCABLE dia. 13"	TRUNNION dia. 4¼"	BORE dia. 5¾"

INFORMATION

Designed like its neighbours by Lt. Gen. William Millar this gun differs in that it is intended for use on land, rather than at sea. The gun has a Gomer chamber and there is a dispart patch on the muzzle. The cascable button is unusual. Although the cutaway portion underneath is clearly intended to receive elevating gear there are various extra holes whose purpose is obscure. It is possible that these holes have been provided in order to fit an experimental sight but without further evidence this cannot be verified.

MARKS ON GUN

Although very worn the marks which can be identified allow the gun to be dated with surprising accuracy. On the chase the cipher of the Secretary of State (S of S) for War, Jonathan Peel, can just be discerned and although it is illegible the outline is sufficient to identify it.

image ©A.L. Boxell (20.08.2008)

After the post of MGO was abolished in 1855 the cipher of the Minister for War appeared on cannons. Peel occupied this post twice, each time for only one year, in 1858 and again in 1866.

Jonathan Peel (1799-1879) left the army with the rank of Lt. General on 4.8.1863. Between 1841 and 1846 he had been Surveyor General of the Ordnance and in 1858 his time as War Minister was cut short when the government fell. His second appointment as S of S for War was also brief as he tendered his resignation rather than support Disraeli's scheme of reform. A Tory, he was popular, honest and of 'irreproachable reputation' (DNB p.403). He was a 'strenuous supporter of enquiries into abuses in all matters of military organisation' (*ibid*) and fortuitously his brief tenures of office allow this gun to be dated very accurately. It was cast in 1858 or 1866.

image ©A.L. Boxell (05.06.2007)

GUN NO. 11 on plan	ACCESSION No./GUN TYPE/ CARRIAGE Accession no. uncertain. British brass 24pdr. SBML.	LOCATION North Bailey right of Keep entrance

MEASUREMENTS

BARREL Length 57" (4'9")	CASCABLE dia. 13"	TRUNNION dia. 4¼"	BORE dia. 5¼"

INFORMATION
The Blomefield loop on the cascable indicates that this gun was intended for use at sea, where a breeching rope passing through the loop and attached at two points to the side of the ship, one on each side of the gun, would restrain the piece during recoil. With the exception of Gun No. 10 all the pieces in this line (7,8,9 and 11) would have been employed as naval ordnance as in 1848. 'All line of battle ships of the 1st, 2nd, and 3rd rate [12] [had] 2 24pounder brass howitzers, 13cwt and 2 12pounder howitzers, light 6cwt for boat service; and 1 6pounder light brass gun for boat service and short practice'. (Douglas p.603)

Like its neighbours the gun has a dispart patch on the muzzle.

MARKS ON GUN
The royal cipher of Queen Victoria is barely visible on the first reinforce. The MGO cipher on the chase is even more worn but a baronial coronet can be discerned. The letter enclosed in the design could be a 'P' and if so it could be the monogram of Lord Panmure (S of S for War 1855 – '58). It is, however, too indistinct to base any judgment upon it.

---

[12] The rating system for naval ships, devised by Samuel Pepys (1633-1703) was an indication of the number of guns carried as armament. A first rate carried a minimum of 100 guns, lower rates less in descending order, the lowest rated being a sixth rate. In fact a warship usually carried more guns than her rating suggested as carronades, invented after the system came into force, were carried on some ships but simply ignored as their inclusion in the count would have upset the rating system.

SOUTHSEA CASTLE

Line of Millar's Guns situated outside the Keep,
consisting of three 12pdrs. and two 24pdrs.
(the black gun at the beginning of the line belongs to the re-enactment Group)

image ©A.L. Boxell (23.05.2007)

SOUTHSEA CASTLE

Gun No. 12

image ©A.L. Boxell (15.06.2007)

image ©A.L. Boxell (15.06.2007)

SOUTHSEA CASTLE

Gun No. 12

image ©A.L. Boxell (15.08.2007)

The Blomefield design was extremely functional, avoiding the flamboyant excesses of previous patterns of cannon. The muzzle design shown here is mentioned in the text.
The small nick halfway down the muzzle is the mark used in ranging the gun by aligning it with the quarter sight marks on the cascable. The quarter sight scale can be seen in the previous photograph and its method of use is explained in the information accompanying gun 18.

GUN NO. 12	ACCESSION No./ GUN TYPE/CARRIAGE 1973/1187/66 Formerly 1187/73/b British 12pdr. cast iron smooth bore gun, Blomefield pattern.	LOCATION Eastern Bailey Left hand gun of two

MEASUREMENTS

BARREL Length 101" (8'5")	CASCABLE dia. 17"	TRUNNION dia 4½"	BORE dia. 4¾"

INFORMATION

This gun was stored at Eastney until 15th February 1978. The Blomefield breeching loop on the cascable identifies it as a sea service gun which must have been cast after 1787, when Blomefield introduced this new design. The vent patch is drilled to receive a flintlock igniter. A 12pdr., the gun seems to be a standard piece of its type, manufactured by the Walker Co. Blomefield's influence on the design can be seen even in the smallest aspects. At the muzzle the use of three simple curves to reduce the muzzle swell down to the face would not actually improve the shooting qualities of the gun but must have simplified casting by eliminating the complicated curves of former designs.

MARKS ON GUN

Some of the marks are now illegible but from records held by the Council it is known that the left trunnion bore the founders mark WC, indicating that the gun was cast by the Walker Co. The right trunnion is marked 50. This would probably be a foundry production number. On the second reinforce the monogram of George III can still be seen and just ahead of this on the chase, there is a square patch in relief marked 26.

This patch would have been part of the sighting system. Smith (p.26) cites a document (WO 47/108) held in the National Archives (formerly Public Record Office) dated January 1787 in which Blomefield gave instructions that "sea service [guns] with loops [were] to have square pieces of metal on the chase."

Later guns of Blomefield design do not have the square patch. Smith suggests that the quarter sight markings replaced this patch. Gun No. 12 has both the patch marked 26 and quarter sights. It is of course possible that the quarter sight markings were a later modification. The method of use of the quarter sights is explained in the information provided about gun No. 18

SOUTHSEA CASTLE

Gun No. 13

image ©A.L. Boxell (15.06.2007)

View looking down the bore showing three groove rifling

image ©A.L. Boxell (15.06.2007)

| GUN NO. 13 | ACCESSION No./GUN TYPE/CARRIAGE British 64pdr. 7" RML or MLR | LOCATION Eastern Bailey. Right hand gun of two. |

MEASUREMENTS

| BARREL Length 109" (9'1") | CASCABLE dia. 21" | TRUNNION dia. 8" | BORE dia. 6⅝" |

INFORMATION
Some confusion exists about the terminology of guns in service circa 1863. When the RN reverted to (rifled) muzzle loading guns in 1865 an attempt was made to utilise some of the larger smooth bore guns by converting them to rifled muzzle loaders (RML) using a system devised by Major Palliser. This was really an interim measure but when new muzzle loaders came into service they were designated MLRs in order to differentiate between the two types. (Moore pp. 26 & 35). Under this system, then, gun 13 should be designated an 'MLR'. This nomenclature seems to have fallen into disuse; it would in any case only have been applicable until 1881, when breech loading ordnance was re-adopted. Both types of gun fired shells rather than spherical shot, employing a rifling system consisting of three concentric grooves cut into the inner surface of the barrel to form a spiral (see photo.). Studs on the outer surface of the shell engaged the grooves which imparted a spin to the projectile thereby increasing its range and accuracy. Although the studded shell on display in the Keep is of a different calibre and would not therefore fit this weapon it does provide a good example of the type of projectile fired by this gun.

There are two vertical holes right through the rear of the jacket flanking a central hole which was probably part of the sighting system. A similar grouping of holes can be seen at trunnion level. Presumably the central holes would have contained the sights while the flanking holes provided some kind of support. Another hole to the right of the central 'sight' hole is filled with a preserving screw.

At the extreme rear end the button is holed to admit the passage of a breeching rope but there is no 'gate' provided for speedy replacement of the rope. The breeching loop indicates that this was, at least originally, a sea service gun.

MARKS ON GUN
The two most interesting marks on this gun are the gouges on the front of the rear jacket which appear to have been made by enemy fire. It is certainly difficult to imagine what else could have caused them, although there is no confirmatory evidence.

Just ahead of the central rear (sight?) hole the weight of the piece (64-1-0) is shown in hundredweights (cwts.), quarters (qrs.) and pounds avoirdupois (lbs.). In front of the touch hole the monogram of Queen Victoria is incised into the top of the jacket. The left trunnion originally showed the date of manufacture (1877) but this is no longer legible.

The right trunnion has two lines which cross one another at a right angle. The horizontal line indicated the axis of the barrel and would have been used to level the gun

image ©A.L. Boxell (30.08.2007)

Above, impact marks on front of rear jacket.
Below, rear view of gun, note preserving screw

image ©A.L. Boxell (30.08.2007)

SOUTHSEA CASTLE

Royal Ciphers used by Queen Victoria.

This Queen enjoyed the longest reign of any English monarch and during her reign (1837-1901) she employed three ciphers. These ciphers are officially registered at the College of Arms and are sometimes attributed dates by historians, who understandably assume that the cipher on a cannon of known date must be the one current at that time. However the College of Arms advise that these ciphers give no indication of date as they were apparently used in haphazard fashion by a variety of users. They are shown below and all three may be seen on guns within the castle.

SOUTHSEA CASTLE

Gun No. 14

image ©A.L. Boxell (30.08.2007)

EL THEOFEO

image ©A.L. Boxell (30.08.2007)

GUN NO. 14 As shown on plan	ACCESSION No./ GUN TYPE/CARRIAGE 1968/303 Spanish SBML Brass 6pdr.	LOCATION Entrance to Caponier and Tunnels

MEASUREMENTS

BARREL Length 64" (5'4") 69½" overall	CASCABLE dia. 10"	TRUNNION dia. 3¼"	BORE dia. 3⅝"

INFORMATION

Purchased in 1968 from a dealer, Charles Perry, with a grant from the V &A. Although this gun, like the other three Spanish 6pounders in the castle, formed part of the armament of the privateer *Louisa,* it differs from its companions in some particulars. It is, for example, some fifteen years older and bears different markings. Essentially, though, it is the same type as the others.

MARKS ON GUN

On the chase the name of the gun, El Theofeo, is not difficult to make out. Unfortunately the other markings on the gun are less easy to read and the difficulty is compounded by the awkward positioning of the piece. Unlike its two neighbours El Theofeo has no marks on the base ring, but on the rear of the cascable the date of manufacture can be discerned as part of the inscription 'JOSEPHUS BARNO LA FECIT BAR 1762'. 'Fecit 1762' certainly means 'made in 1762' but any translation of the rest of the inscription could only be speculative, even for speakers of Spanish.[13]

On the right trunnion the marks are somewhat indistinct but appear to be $7q^s\,54L$. These would be the weight of the piece (7quintals 54libra) while underneath the abbreviation 'PE^o' means 'peso' (weight). The final mark 'OAS' or 'QAS' is not comprehensible.

The left trunnion is very worn but the top line of the text appears to be 'BRONCE 8' and the last 'MERICA'. 'Bronce' is Spanish for 'bronze'

Surprisingly the gun does not bear the cipher of Charles III (King from 1759 to 1788) despite being cast during his occupation of the throne. This might indicate that it was not intended for service in the Spanish armed forces.

---

[13] While the base ring markings of the neighbouring Spanish guns (Latino and Grillo) appear to be written in Spanish, the inscription on El Theofeo seems to be Latin. 'Fecit' is definitely Latin for 'made' and it was quite common to find this word, followed by the date, even on early English guns. Josephus Barno (or Barnola) is probably the founder's name. Barno sounds improbable but it may be an abbreviation. The 'BAR' before that date is also an abbreviation, probably for Barcelona. This would explain the different position of the marks on this gun when compared to the other two, which were cast in Seville. Bearing all this in mind a suggested translation would be 'made by Joseph Barno(la) in Barcelona in 1762'.

SOUTHSEA CASTLE

Gun No. 14
Theofeo – inscription on cascable

image ©A.L. Boxell (30.08.2007)

Gun 14	Gun 15	Gun 16
El Theofeo	Latino	Grillo

image ©A.L. Boxell (30.08.2007)

GUN NO. 15	ACCESSION No./ GUN TYPE/CARRIAGE	LOCATION
	1968/301 Spanish SBML Brass 6pdr.	Entrance to Caponier and tunnels

MEASUREMENTS

BARREL Length 64" (5'4") 69½" overall	CASCABLE dia. 10"	TRUNNION dia. 3¼"	BORE dia. 3⅝"

INFORMATION

Purchased from Charles Perry in 1968 this gun, like its neighbours, formed part of the complement of the Craven family's privateer *Louisa*.[14] Of Spanish origin, this brass smooth bore muzzle loader fired a 6 pound cannonball which would be fairly negligible in naval terms but no doubt proved sufficient to overcome the merchant ships on which the *Louisa* would have preyed.

An unusual feature of all four of these Spanish guns is the lack of a second reinforce. Ahead of the vent field the first reinforce extends beyond the trunnions, after which it cuts to the chase, (no pun intended – well, only partly intended). This could possibly be a feature of small calibre Spanish guns. A Spanish 18Pdr. of similar date held at the Tower of London has the normal configuration (Blackmore XIX.89 'Arion' p. 147) so presumably the lack of a second reinforce was not a feature which applied to all Spanish guns.

MARKS ON GUN

On the base ring the casting date and foundry of origin are very clear. Sevilla 31 De Octubre de 1776. The monogram of Charles III of Spain occupies most of the first reinforce and ahead of this, at the muzzle end of the chase, the name of the gun "Latino" is inscribed on a scroll. On the right trunnion the inscription P⁰770 indicates the weight (peso) of the piece. As the quintal approximated 100lbs. this inscription could be read as either 7quintals 70pounds (libra) or 770pounds.[15]

---

[14] Privateers were 'privately owned ships commissioned to act as warships against a hostile power'. (Howarth p.133) Operating with a 'letter of marque' from the sovereign they could claim royal protection if captured and with luck could avoid being treated as pirates. Francis Drake was probably the best known of Elizabethan privateers, although strictly speaking his early operations on the Spanish Main were not truly privateering, as Spain could not at that time be termed a 'hostile power'. Nevertheless provided his behaviour was not too outrageous the Queen was prepared to share his booty which after all had only been taken from Spaniards who had themselves plundered it from others.
Privateering was not confined to English seamen. The French had their corsairs the most famous of whom, Jacques Cartier, not only gave Canada its name but subsequently seems to have had half of Quebec named after himself.

[15] Research shows that the quintal is variously described as being equivalent to 100 kilograms under the metric system, or equal to 100 pounds in the United States. If the former conversion is accepted these Spanish guns would each weigh some 15cwt., or three quarters of a ton. Having personally moved the guns by hand the author considers that the latter conversion rate is more reasonable.

Charles III of Spain (1716-1788, King from 1759) was the son of Philip V and his wife Elizabeth Farnese. During his reign he made serious attempts to improve the efficiency of the Army and the administration. He was responsible also for improvements in educational standards, and he encouraged the growth of trade and industry. His reign was also notable for the expulsion of the Jesuits from Spain and its Empire in 1767. Charles was formerly King of Naples but left this possession to his son Ferdinand on becoming King of Spain in 1759. (New Caxton Encyclopedia p.1266).

During Charles's reign Britain and Spain were at war twice. In the brief war of 1762/3 the Spanish were driven out of Portugal and under the Treaty of Paris which ended the war Spain lost a number of islands in the West Indies to Britain. In 1779 Spain joined America, France and Holland in another war against Britain, unsuccessfully laying siege to Gibraltar and suffering a heavy Naval defeat off Cape St. Vincent. Under the Treaty of Versailles in 1783 Spain regained Florida and Minorca but Britain retained its possession of Gibraltar

image ©A.L. Boxell (15.06.2007)

This empirical opinion is confirmed by Blackmore (p.148) who states quintal equals "100lbs".Consequently throughout this book a quintal is considered to be roughly equivalent to 100lbs avoirdupois.

CHARLES III KING OF SPAIN 1759 – 1788

A contemporary painting by an unknown artist

SOUTHSEA CASTLE

Gun No. 16

Name of the gun marked on the chase

image ©A.L. Boxell (03.07.2007)

Marks on left trunnion, probably the gun's serial number.

image ©A.L. Boxell (24.07.2007)

GUN NO. 16 on plan	ACCESSION No./ GUN TYPE/CARRIAGE 1968/302 Spanish SBML Brass 6pdr	LOCATION Entrance to Caponier and Tunnels

MEASUREMENTS

BARREL Length 64" (5'4") 69½" overall	CASCABLE dia. 10"	TRUNNION dia. 3¼"	BORE dia. 3⅝"

INFORMATION
Similar in most respects to the other Spanish 6pounders on display this gun is the last to be seen before entering the tunnels. It was cast in Seville in 1776 and eventually formed part of the armament of the privateer *Louisa*.

MARKS ON GUN
On the base ring the place and date of casting are given as 'Sevilla 19 De Septiembre De 1776'. The first reinforce has the monogram of Charles III of Spain incised and further up the barrel, near the muzzle, the name of the gun (Grillo) is inscribed on a scroll. The trunnion markings are rather less clear but the weight of the piece (P^o 780) can be made out on the right while the left has the figure 470. This latter figure is preceded by a weird squiggle similar to that found on gun no. 6 (Fiera). The figures are probably the production number but the squiggle is indecipherable.

CARRIAGE
While the carriages of all three Spanish guns located in the entrance to the tunnels are similar they are described on the provenance as 'old' but not 'original'. Whether this means that the carriages were not the original ones on which the guns were mounted or that, although old, they are reproductions is not clear. They are, however, somewhat singular in design in that the trunnion holes are located slightly forward of the front trucks (wheels). What effect this would have when firing the gun can only be surmised but the design certainly gives an impression of imbalance to the piece. One effect is that if downward pressure is exerted on the gun at the muzzle end the rear trucks are lifted off the ground. This does not happen when the same test is applied to the similar gun 6 (Fiera) which is mounted on a conventional carriage.

SOUTHSEA CASTLE

Gun No. 17

Photographs shown by kind permission of the Board of Trustees of the Royal Armouries

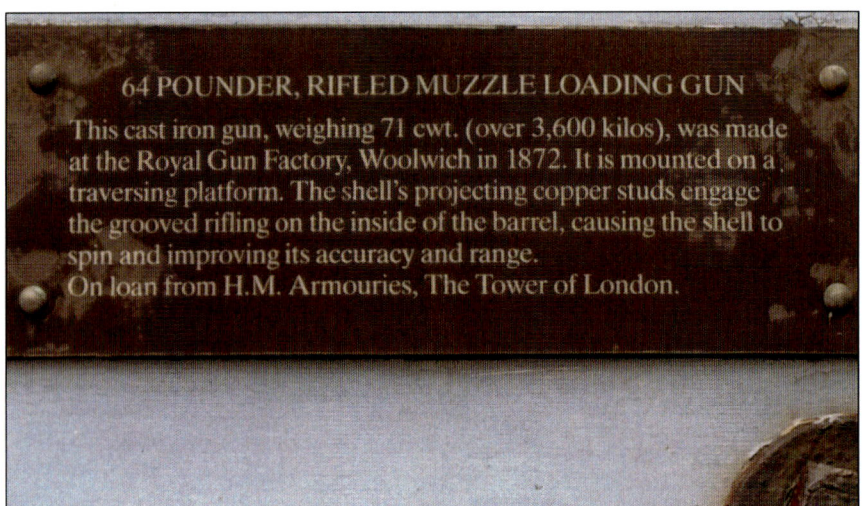

64 POUNDER, RIFLED MUZZLE LOADING GUN

This cast iron gun, weighing 71 cwt. (over 3,600 kilos), was made at the Royal Gun Factory, Woolwich in 1872. It is mounted on a traversing platform. The shell's projecting copper studs engage the grooved rifling on the inside of the barrel, causing the shell to spin and improving its accuracy and range.
On loan from H.M. Armouries, The Tower of London.

GUN NO. 17 on plan	ACCESSION No./ GUN TYPE/CARRIAGE 1966/41 British 64pdr/8" RML (converted) gun of 71cwt. on wooden sliding carriage and traversing platform	LOCATION South Platform

MEASUREMENTS

BARREL Length 9' 3"	CASCABLE dia. 22"	TRUNNION dia. 7"	BORE dia. 6¼"

INFORMATION

This gun (XIX.650) has been on loan from the Royal Armouries since 1964. It was originally a 32pdr. SBML but in 1872 it was converted into a rifled muzzle loader (RML) under the Palliser system.[16] This conversion, which was carried out at the Royal Gun Factory (RGF) at Woolwich, transformed the weapon from a smooth bored muzzle loader firing a 32 pound cannonball into a rifled gun firing a 64 pound shell. This was accomplished by boring out the barrel then inserting a coiled wrought iron rifled liner. As their external dimensions remained the same any gun converted under the Palliser system could still be mounted on its original carriage. When a converted gun was re-mounted on a truck carriage in order to cope with the increased recoil generated by the 64lb shell a braking device known as 'Allen's Brake' was brought into service which, when attached, in effect chocked the front trucks (wheels) of the carriage, thus restricting their rearward movement. This braking system could not be employed on a sliding carriage of the type seen here.

While the wooden carriage and traversing platform on which gun 17 is mounted are only replicas they do show how these coastal defence guns were used operationally. The curved racers (see glossary) allowed the guns to be traversed widely so that they had interlocking arcs of fire. The rear pivot is actually made from a cannibalised barrel. Similar pivots can be seen at other points around the castle but sadly only this one now performs its original function. The platform on which the gun rests is angled upward towards the rear in order to lessen the effect of recoil and the friction generated by the chocks as they recoiled would also have helped in this respect.

MARKS ON GUN

On the left trunnion the marks RGF N⁰ 709 1872 are quite clear, providing the serial no. of the gun together with its date of manufacture at the Royal Gun Factory at Woolwich. On the face of the muzzle the marks RGF 1 which were formerly incised can no longer be seen. Comparison with other converted guns elsewhere indicates that this muzzle marking would originally have been RGF IRON, presumably used to differentiate between those guns with wrought iron rifled barrel liners and those in which steel inserts were used.[17]

---

[16] See INFORMATION on page 47

[17] Although there were numerous attempts by foreign nations to rifle cast-iron ordnance 'The only methods by which cast iron was ever successfully used for rifled guns were those proposed by Sir W. Palliser (1863) and Mr. Parsons (1860), who inserted, the one, a coiled wrought-iron, and the other, a steel tube, in a cast-iron body. Large numbers of cast-iron smooth-bore guns were by *these* methods [author's italics] converted into rifled guns' (Lloyd and Hadcock p. 41) Perhaps Palliser's subsequent Knighthood (he was originally a Major) and Parson's lack of this honour indicates the success of their respective methods.

SOUTHSEA CASTLE

Gun No. 17

Photographs shown by kind permission of the Board of Trustees of the Royal Armouries

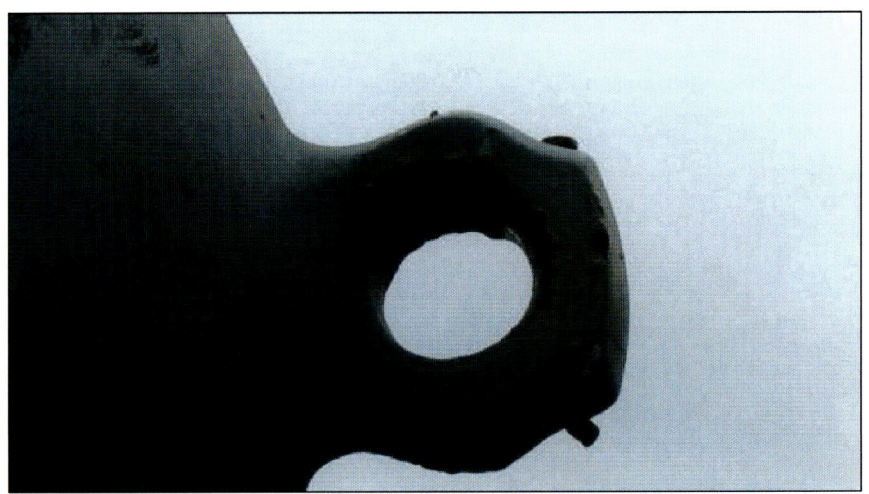

The replica carriage on which gun 17 is mounted is deficient in some respects. The runners, for instance, should be thicker and the front fittings which are angled towards the front of the slide are intended to support wheels. On this carriage the wheels are missing which gives a false impression of the mechanics involved in operating the gun. The photograph below (taken at Fort Nelson and shown by kind permission of the Board of Trustees of the Royal Armouries) shows how these wheels were attached. Note also the central part of the carriage which is restrained on either side by the cheeks of the slide, thus preventing lateral movement of the gun when it recoils and holding it in position on the mounting.

image ©A.L. Boxell (11.10.2007)

The frictional force of the chocks against the slide which helped tame the recoil of the gun had to be overcome in order to run the gun forward to its firing position after reloading, and the drawing on the following page shows how this was accomplished. The combination of wheels and chocks enabled the gun to be operated with comparative ease despite its weight but even so prolonged firing would still be exhausting for the crew who were now required to handle a 64pound shell, rather than the 32pound cannon ball formerly fired by this gun

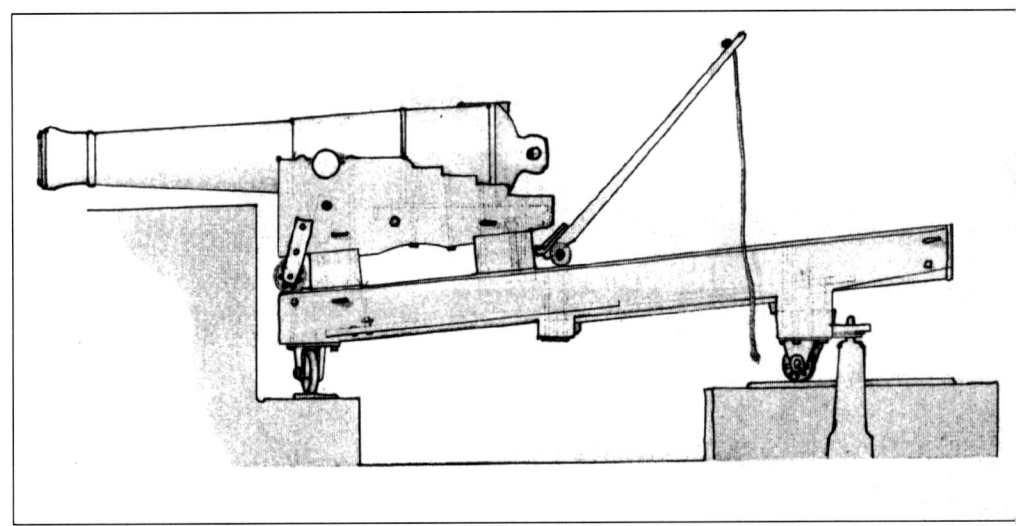
Sliding carriage mounted on the traversing Platform. Method of Use

SOUTHSEA CASTLE

Gun No. 17
Rear views of replica carriage

Photographs shown by kind permission of the Board of Trustees of the Royal Armouries

SOUTHSEA CASTLE

Gun No. 18

image ©A.L. Boxell (04.07.2007)

Cannon balls at side are not the correct size for this gun

image ©A.L. Boxell (04.07.2007)

GUN NO. 18 on plan	ACCESSION No./ GUN TYPE/CARRIAGE 1962/23/2 (formerly 23/62/A) British 32pdr. cast iron SBML on cast iron garrison carriage.	LOCATION East Platform

MEASUREMENTS

BARREL Length 9'3"	CASCABLE dia. 22"	TRUNNION dia. 6⅜"	BORE dia. 6¼"

INFORMATION
This gun and its neighbour on the East Platform were obtained by the Council in 1962 through the good offices of Lt. Col. Tobin, who at that time was the Commanding Officer of the Regimental Depot at Hilsea Barracks. It is a fine example of the Blomefield pattern 32pounder and was cast by the Walker Company. The breeching loop above the button immediately identifies the gun as a Blomefield design and gives some indication of its casting date, as the loop was not adopted until 1787. The Walker Co., was the first foundry to cast the looped guns but this particular gun is obviously of later date, as its number indicates. Bloomfield's influence on the design can also be seen in the smooth cascable, already discussed in the text for gun no. 1.

On the very bottom of the cascable the weight of the piece (55-1-14) is shown in hundredweights, quarters and pounds avoirdupois (cwts., qrs., and lbs.).

Just forward of the cascable, on top of the vent field, a raised vent patch is drilled laterally to take a flintlock igniter. There were several types of these igniters but all worked in the same way. A piece of flint was driven forward onto the frizzen plate causing a shower of sparks to be directed onto the quill primer, igniting it and causing it, in its turn, to ignite the main charge through the touch hole.[18]

MARKS ON GUN
On top of the loop the letters CV stand for 'Copper Vent', indicating that the gun has been bushed (from the French '*bouched*') with a copper insert. This entailed tapping the vent then screwing in a copper bush which had a hole already drilled in the centre.[19] This repair would sometimes be necessary because when the gun was fired some of the hot gas created by the explosion escaped up the vent. Over a period of time this occurrence would cause an erosion of the metal surrounding the vent, enlarging it eventually to the point where the gun would become unserviceable.[20] Bushing was introduced around 1785 and copper was employed as it could withstand the erosion better than other metals.

---

[18] The 'touch hole' is the vent orifice; that part of the vent where the charge was fired, or 'touched off'. The term touch hole may be unofficial, but it was certainly in use by 18th century gunners. (RNM Mss 1988/41/1 pp.19 and 22)

[19] Improvised methods of bushing in the field were not unknown. At the siege of Badajoz in the Peninsular campaign Lt. Col. Alexander Dickson bushed some guns by filling their enlarged vent holes with molten copper then drilling new vents through it. (Hughes p. 22).

[20] The normal size vent in British Service was 0.2"

SOUTHSEA CASTLE

Gun No. 18
Looped cascable, quarter sight scale and raised vent patch

image ©A.L. Boxell (26.08.2008)

Foundry mark on trunnion

image ©A.L. Boxell (26.08.2008)

Between 1844 and 1855 iron bushes were used but their use was discontinued as they were found to be less effective than those made of copper. Guns with iron bushes were marked IV (iron vent). After 1855 all newly manufactured guns were bushed with copper prior to issue. Presumably from this date the CV marking would no longer be required.

Around the edge of the cascable on each side are thirteen equal gradations. These are the 'quarter sights', so called because each mark above the base mark, when aligned with the mark at the side of the muzzle, would raise the barrel a quarter of a degree. The barrel on these naval guns could only be raised at sea to a maximum of three degrees as any elevation in excess of that might cause the recoiling barrel to contact the top of the ship's gun port. The marks at the muzzle (one on each side), being halfway down the circumference of the barrel, meant that when the gun-layer aligned the muzzle mark with the lowest gradation of the quarter sights his line of sight was at the same level as the axis of the barrel. By dropping the rear of the barrel any of the quarter sight gradations could be similarly aligned until the gun attained its maximum effective range.[21]

On land, of course, the gun could be elevated much more than three degrees but in this circumstance the quarter sight would obviously not be used.

A broad arrow is incised on the first reinforce and on the top of the second reinforce, between the trunnions, the monogram of George III is in relief. Just ahead of this at the start of the chase a raised sight patch can be seen. On the left trunnion the letters W. C° are incised, showing that the gun was cast by the Walker Co. The right trunnion bears the serial no. of the gun, 648.

The pile of shot adjacent to the gun is of smaller calibre than a 32pdr., but does give some idea of the lethality of the weaponry employed at the beginning of the 19th century. (The historical period can be deduced by estimating the age of the gun which must have been cast between 1787, when the breeching loop first appeared, and 1820 when George III died).

CARRIAGE
The gun is mounted on an iron garrison carriage which, as the name implies, was not intended for use at sea. This type of iron carriage was particularly useful in foreign garrisons where wooden carriages could be more prone to damage arising from attack by insects or the excesses of tropical weather.

It is interesting to note that the main support strut subtends an angle of 30°. This would be approximately the angle of elevation required for the gun to achieve its maximum

---

[21] The quarter 'sights' were in fact only an indication of the elevation of the gun. A sight, properly so called, would imply that by correctly aligning three points (rear sight, fore sight and target) the shooter could actually be confident of hitting his target. This alignment could never usefully be achieved by the use of quarter sights as the cascable was wider than the muzzle of the gun. Aligning quarter sights with a target would therefore cause a lateral deviation of some magnitude even at the short ranges at which naval engagements of the time were fought. Eventually, of course, the range attained by a naval artillery piece would far exceed the visual range of the gunners but this was not the case in the early 19th century, when most engagements at sea occurred at point blank range.

range,[22] using its heaviest charge to enable it to do so. The main strength of the carriage is thus opposed to the line of maximum recoil thrust.

On the left cheek piece of the carriage the inscription 32P^R can be seen flanking the government broad arrow, while further to the rear the weight of the carriage is given as 22-3-16. Between these two sets of marks N.4 is incised. The 32P^R mark is repeated on the opposite side of the carriage. These marks accentuate the difference between this type of garrison carriage and the skeletal type on which gun no. 1 is mounted. Whereas the skeletal type can be adapted to accommodate a number of different calibre guns the 32pounder carriage can not, as the marking implies.

image ©A.L. Boxell (04.05.2005)

[22] Although a projectile travelling *in a vacuum* would achieve its maximum range if fired at an elevation of 45° this is not the case when the projectile travels through a resisting medium such as air. Air resistance affects the projectile in such a way that it needs to make distance in the earlier part of its trajectory, as the resistance has the greatest effect when the velocity of the projectile is at its maximum. Because the speed of the projectile diminishes throughout its flight the ascending and descending branches of the trajectory are not similar to each other, so the trajectory will always be in the form of a parabola. It has been found by experimentation that 'in proportion as the initial velocity is diminished, the angle [of departure] which gives the maximum range is greater'. (Douglas p. 66) Simply put this means that in order to achieve its maximum range a cricket ball should be thrown at roughly 45° whereas a gun would need to be fired at roughly 30° in order to achieve its maximum range.

BUSHING THE VENT

As already described in the text accompanying gun 18 the gas escaping up the vent on firing would eventually erode the metal, enlarging the vent and resulting in the gun becoming inoperable. This could sometimes be dangerous to the gun crew as sometimes the bush would be blown out of the gun but good maintenance should prevent this. The normal size vent was 0.2" and regular gauging should give some warning of the development of a dangerous situation but this would not always be possible in prolonged periods of action. After the siege of Badajoz there were several complaints of guns becoming unbushed, as more British guns became inoperable from this cause than through enemy action.

It may come as a surprise to realize just how much gas escaped through the vent on firing. This back pressure had considerable force. When Samuel Pepys returned to England as part of the party which accompanied the Prince of Orange from Holland he became involved in the general celebrations which greeted the Prince's return and actually fired one of the saluting guns himself. He recorded in his famous diary (22:5:1660) that "holding my head too much over the gun, I had almost spoiled my right eye". The picture below gives some idea of the force of the back blast.

The following marks on the loop of the cascable indicated the type of bushing employed

CV = Copper Vent   IV = Iron Vent
N   = New (gun)
C   = Cone   TV = Through Vent

Photo taken at Fort Nelson and shown by kind permission of
Board of Trustees of Royal Armouries

SOUTHSEA CASTLE

Gun No. 19

image ©A.L. Boxell (25.08.2007)

image ©A.L. Boxell (25.08.2007)

GUN NO. 19 on plan	ACCESSION No./ GUN TYPE/CARRIAGE 1962/23/3 (formerly 23/62/D) British 32pdr. cast iron SBML gun on cast iron garrison carriage	LOCATION East Platform

MEASUREMENTS

BARREL Length 9'3"	CASCABLE dia. 22"	TRUNNION dia. 6⅜"	BORE dia. 6¼"

INFORMATION
This 32pdr., is identical to its companion, gun No. 18, which stands alongside it on the East Platform. It was obtained by the Council at the same time as its neighbour and probably came from the same source at Hilsea Barracks. Certainly it was cast in the Walker Co., foundry but probably rather earlier than its companion if a comparison of the respective serial numbers is any criterion.

MARKS ON GUN
On the bottom of the cascable the weight of the gun is shown as 55-3-18. This positioning is unusual as the weight of a piece is often more visible, usually being located on the top of the gun. It would be comforting to suppose that the position of the weight marks on a Walker gun could differentiate between those cast at Rotherham prior to 1817 and those cast after 1820 at Tipton. Unfortunately the facts do not support this theory.

The Walker Co., logo is shown on the left trunnion[23] and on the right the serial no. 267 appears. CVC on the loop of the cascable indicates that the gun has a copper vent. The royal monogram of George III is on top of the first reinforce with a broad arrow nearer the vent. The shot piled near the gun are too small for it.

CARRIAGE
The iron garrison carriage has its weight (23-0-8) marked on the left cheek piece. Apart from the 20lb. difference in weight the carriage is identical to its neighbour.

The design of this type of carriage is attributed to Stephen Remnant. Presumably this was the same Stephen Remnant who had a forge at the Royal Dockyard and contracted to cast the railings for the Verbruggen's renovation of the Royal Brass Foundry in 1773. (Jackson & De Beer. pp 42/45).

---

[23] For a brief history of the Walker Co., see text on Gun No. 1.

SOUTHSEA CASTLE

Left to right – Guns Nos. 20, 21 and 22

image ©A.L. Boxell (05.04.2007)

Foundry mark on right trunnion

image ©A.L. Boxell (05.04.2007)

GUN NO. 20 On plan	ACCESSION No./ GUN TYPE/CARRIAGE Possibly 1973/1189 British 32pdr. cast iron SBML	LOCATION North Platform nearest lighthouse

MEASUREMENTS

BARREL Length 9'0"	CASCABLE dia. 22"	TRUNNION dia. 6⅜"	BORE dia. 6¼" (approx.)

INFORMATION
This gun, like the two similar guns to its right on the north platform, was probably purchased by the Council in 1973 with the help of a V & A purchase grant. Like its companions also it was probably one of the guns found on the *Foudroyant*. Cast at the Low Moor Iron Co. in Bradford, Yorks., it is a Dixon/Dundas pattern 32pdr. SBML. It has two small holes on the chase which are probably for the attachment of a sight. A raised vent rib provides an attachment for a gunlock. The breeching loop has been lowered to pierce the button and it features a removable gate held by a pin. The diameter of the bore could not be accurately measured owing to the position of the piece so it was estimated using the size of the nearby cannonballs as a guide. These may very well not be the correct size for the gun so this information should be treated with caution.

The designer of these guns. Lt. Col. William Dundas, was the Inspector of Artillery at Woolwich (1839 – 1852). His major achievement was the 68pdr. of 95cwt. which was first cast in 1847 and threw the heaviest solid shot fired from a smooth-bore naval gun. According to Caruana, however, Dundas's 32pdr. design contained a 'fatal flaw' in that it did not eradicate a 'plane of weakness in the area of greatest pressure' (Caruana (2) pp 13/14). This weak point was embodied in the 1838 design of Mr. Monk, the chief clerk of the RGF and by restricting his design to the external pattern introduced by Millar, (another of his predecessors) Dundas failed to rectify Monk's inherent fault.[24]

MARKS ON GUN
Very few marks are visible. On the right trunnion the foundry name Low Moor can be discerned and on the chase the Victorian royal cipher is shown in relief. There are no quarter sight markings (it appears there never were any) and the MGO's cipher is also missing. The date and weight were originally shown on the first reinforce but are now illegible.

---

[24] It is probable that Dundas was unaware of the 'plane of weakness' incorporated in Monk's design. This knowledge was published by Robert Mallet in 1856 and the last British designer of smooth bore muzzle loaders, Francis Eardley Wilmot used this knowledge to produce his 1857 design. It is not certain that Wilmot's guns were ever cast owing to the introduction of the compound gun in 1859 (Caruana (2) p. 14) which marked the end of the use of smooth bore muzzle loaders in the British service.

SOUTHSEA CASTLE

Gun No. 21

image ©A.L. Boxell (18.07.2005)

Cipher of Queen Victoria in relief between trunnions

image ©A.L. Boxell (31.08.2006)

GUN NO. 21　On plan	ACCESSION No./ GUN TYPE/CARRIAGE　1973/1190 British 32pdr. cast iron SBML on wooden garrison carriage.	LOCATION　North Platform　2nd clockwise from lighthouse.

MEASUREMENTS

BARREL Length　9'0"	CASCABLE dia.　22"	TRUNNION dia.　6⅜"	BORE dia.　6¼"

INFORMATION
This Dixon/Dundas gun, the central one of three, was bought with the aid of a V & A purchase grant. Another ex *Foudroyant* gun it is similar in most respects to those that flank it but is not so corroded as gun no. 20.

MARKS ON GUN
On the left trunnion the number 2639 would be the serial number while on the other trunnion the foundry is identified as Low Moor. The letters CV on the loop of the button, standing for 'copper vent', show that the gun has been bushed, (as described elsewhere in this book). The Royal Cipher of Queen Victoria is in relief between the trunnions but all other marks such as the broad arrow nearby have been engraved. This indicates that the foundry was employing a manufacturing method whereby virtually the whole length of the gun could be cleaned up by turning. As the trunnion area could not be turned any relief ornamentation would conveniently be placed at that level while any marks on turned surfaces would be engraved. This simplification of design not only increased productivity but must have increased profitability as well. The weight of the gun is given as 60-2-10 which appears to make it approximately half a ton heavier than gun no. 22. This might be because of a misreading.

Another puzzling mark is the date, which is shown on the reinforce as 1844. According to Kennard the Low Moor Iron Co. was founded in 1788 by Richard Hird, Joseph Dawson and John Hardy. The firm started gun production in 1791 and continued until the end of the Napoleonic Wars (1815). The firm did not resume gun production until the outbreak of the Crimean War (1854-56) and finally ceased iron gun production after the Indian mutiny, (1858) so a casting date of 1844 is anomalous.

SOUTHSEA CASTLE

Gun No. 22

This gun guards the entrance to the castle. It is situated immediately over the gate with its muzzle just above the royal coat of arms of Charles the second.

image ©A.L. Boxell (05.04.2007)

GUN NO. 22	ACCESSION No./ GUN TYPE/CARRIAGE	LOCATION
On plan	1973/1191 British 32pdr. cast iron SBML on wooden garrison carriage.	North Platform 3rd clockwise from lighthouse.

MEASUREMENTS

BARREL Length	CASCABLE dia.	TRUNNION dia.	BORE dia.
9'0"	22"	6⅜"	6¼"

INFORMATION

The third Low Moor, Dundas pattern gun overlooks the entrance to the castle. It differs from the others only in the marks on it and, if the figures are to be believed, in weight. The gun has a pierced button with a gate and pin to facilitate breeching rope renewal.

MARKS ON GUN

This gun is marked 1855 on the reinforce and unlike the other Low Moor guns it does not have the CV marking on the button. This tallies with the information (gun 18) provided about vent bushing. On the left trunnion the serial number 6532 appears and Low Moor is marked on the right trunnion. Queen Victoria's cipher is in relief between the trunnions and a broad arrow is engraved farther back. The weight in cwts. qrs. and lbs. is given as 50 -1-0.

image ©A.L. Boxell (17.09.2008)

SOUTHSEA CASTLE

Gun No. 23

Photographs shown by kind permission of the Board of Trustees of the Royal Armouries

GUN NO. 23 on plan XIX.653	ACCESSION No./ GUN TYPE/CARRIAGE 1964/74 Russian 18pdr. SBML on repro. Garrison Carriage	LOCATION North platform

MEASUREMENTS

BARREL length 113" (9' 5")	CASCABLE dia. 20"	TRUNNION dia. 5½"	BORE dia. 5½"[25]

INFORMATION

This cast iron SBML is believed to be a Russian 18pounder. On loan from the Royal Armouries since 1964 it was formerly at the Musketry School, Purfleet. For a considerable time it was not accessible to the public because of restorative work, which mainly concerned the construction of a wooden garrison carriage.

The Russian origin of this piece is suggested by the horizontal elevating ring and the flaring muzzle. The left trunnion appears to have been knocked off and re-welded.

MARKS ON GUN

There are no distinguishing marks on the gun.

CARRIAGE

The repro. carriage on which the gun is now mounted was made by a local group of enthusiasts.

---

[25]. The bore diameter was not accessible owing to the position of the piece; it is assumed to be the same size as the trunnion.

SOUTHSEA CASTLE

Gun No. 24

Photographs shown by kind permission of the Board of Trustees of the Royal Armouries

GUN NO. 24 on plan	ACCESSION No./ GUN TYPE/CARRIAGE 1964/73 H 3.2 French 8pdr. SBML	LOCATION North Platform 5th gun clockwise from lighthouse

MEASUREMENTS

BARREL Length104" (8'8")	CASCABLE dia. 20"	TRUNNION dia. 5½"	BORE dia. 4"

INFORMATION

This gun is on loan from the Royal Armouries and is described in the Tower of London catalogue, (gun no.150, p.124 XIX.265). The catalogue describes the gun as an example of the *short* 8pdr. gun of the 1786 series of French naval guns, recording the barrel length as 7'4". This appears to be an error as the length of the barrel is actually 8'8" which would make the gun a *long* 8pdr., of the système 1786. (Boudriot p.87). The gun has a very chequered history as it has been used as a bollard in the Blackfriars district of London. Rescued from this usage by the Royal Armouries it was first lent to the Musketry School at Purfleet before being transferred, still on loan, to its present position.

The système 1786 was a successful design which armed the French navy of the Revolutionary and Napoleonic wars and all French ships until the Restoration. Wishing to replace the guns of the 1778 pattern which were excessively weighty the Minister for the Navy, Marshal de Castries, employed the talents of General Jacques Charles de Manson in designing the 1786 pattern. De Manson was a competent designer who had already been jointly responsible with Gribeauval for the development of the new French land service pattern of ordnance. After touring the three main dockyards and consulting the Navy Councils de Manson produced his successful system.

The noticeable differences are that the système 1786 button is larger and more circular than the previous design while the vent is pear shaped in appearance, having a long shallow pan in front of the vent hole. When filled with gunpowder this pan would facilitate ignition by providing a larger area of contact between the powder and the linstock. In 1810 a modification was introduced and any guns of 1786 pattern made after that date would have been cast with a raised vent patch to support a gunlock.[26] (Boudriot p.81).

There is no second reinforce as the new design lacks the astragal normally found just to the rear of the trunnions, the trunnions themselves are supported by a shoulder and the

---

[26] This evidence militates against the theory sometimes expressed that the combined fleet was equipped with gunlocks at Trafalgar in 1805. The most likely version of events would seem to be that the French introduced this modification in 1810 in a belated attempt to bring their weaponry up to the standard of the Royal Navy.

SOUTHSEA CASTLE

Gun No. 24
Enhanced view of left trunnion.

Marks on right trunnion

Photographs shown by kind permission of the Board of Trustees of the Royal Armouries.

astragal formerly seen at the neck of the muzzle swell has been replaced in the système 1786 by a plain ring.[27]

The gun was cast at Ruelle (in the Charente region near Rochefort), which was one of the main French foundries of the time.

MARKS ON GUN

Doubtless owing to its former employment as a bollard the gun is very corroded and most of the marks mentioned in various sources are no longer apparent. The year of casting and the foundry as originally incised on the base ring are not now legible and even in the 1960s when recorded by Blackmore (p.124) they could only be discerned as AN??? RU[ELLE]. This appears to be a casting date using the French Revolutionary Calendar which would place it between 22nd September 1792 when the calendar was introduced and 1st January 1806 when Napoleon restored the Gregorian calendar.

The left trunnion is marked with the number 424 but the right trunnion marks are less clear, appearing to be either 1812 (the weight in lbs?) or J812 or J8127. The reader may make up his own mind by consulting the enhanced photographs accompanying this text. The reinforce at trunnion level has been engraved with an anchor, flanked by the letters RF (République Française) and surmounted by what could possibly be a 'Bonnet Phrygien',[28] but is even more likely to be a representation of the shapeless hat worn by many *matelots* of the period. This was simply a knitted stocking cap, usually red in colour, which had been introduced into America by the French Voyagers as early as the 16th century. It is known, for example, that Jacques Cartier presented one as a gift to a chief of the Huron tribe. This form of ordinary Breton headgear has also always had connotations of liberty and revolt in France stemming from various disturbances such as the 'revolt of the red caps' in Brittany in 1675, and its adoption by many patriots in the American Revolution of 1775 where it was known as the 'Liberty cap' enhanced this reputation. It was adopted as a national symbol by the French Convention in 1792 but was progressively removed from national monuments during the Consulate (1799-1804) which had been established by a coup d'État.

It is alleged that Napoleon disliked the red cap and as First Consul it is understandable that, having seized power, he would look askance at symbols of revolutionary fervour such as the liberty cap. Assuming all the statements above to be true, they pose an intriguing question. Surely such ciphers on guns would have been removed as part of the Consulate's determination to rid itself of this image, so how did this particular gun survive intact?

---

[27] For much of the information about the French système 1786 I am indebted to Jean Boudriot, whose excellent article on French sea service guns (*vol. 8 Journal of the Ordnance Society*) proved extremely valuable. Other information came from Blackmore's *Tower of London catalogue* and Portsmouth Council's records.

[28] The Bonnet Phrygien was a hat adopted by many French Revolutionaries in the summer of 1790. It became a symbol of the French revolution. Its shape is rather more pronounced than the representation shown on the gun, as the bonnet resembles the hat worn by Punch in the well known puppet show. Possibly, therefore it is likely that the cipher on the gun is intended to represent the hat worn by the ordinary seaman..

SOUTHSEA CASTLE

Gun No. 24
Captured French gun against a backdrop of
Naval War Memorial and Spinnaker Tower.

These pictures shown by kind permission of the Board of Trustees of the Royal Armouries

A theory which fits all the facts and assumptions[29] above is that this gun was cast in 1792/3 at Ruelle, and was subsequently captured in the battle off Brest on 1-6-1794 (the Glorious First of June) thereby avoiding mutilation under the Consulate. If so the gun would certainly be rare and might even be unique.

What is certain is that the gun must have been cast between 1786 when this système was introduced and 1804, as after that date it would have borne the Napoleonic cipher.

Photo below shown by kind permission of the Board of Trustees of the Royal Armouries

image ©A.L. Boxell (25.09.2007)

THE FRENCH REPUBLICAN NAVAL CIPHER.

The author argues that the object surmounting the anchor
is a representation of the revolutionary 'liberty cap' which
became a symbol of revolutionary fervour.

---

[29] Some of the statements about the liberty cap were obtained from the internet so the degree of academic rigour employed by their writers cannot be checked. Jacques Cartier's gift of a hat to the Huron chief is mentioned in a short film shown as part of the guided tour around the Manoir Jacques Cartier at St. Malo in Brittany.

SOUTHSEA CASTLE

Gun No. 25

A Victorian 9 pounder, this gun is similar to gun no. 3.

image ©A.L. Boxell (26.04.2007)

image ©A.L. Boxell (26.04.2007)

| GUN NO. 25 | ACCESSION No./ GUN TYPE/CARRIAGE | LOCATION |
| On plan | 1970/547 British 9pdr. RML on naval travelling carriage. | West Platform |

MEASUREMENTS

BARREL Length	CASCABLE dia.	TRUNNION dia.	BORE dia.
5' 7"	9"	3½"	3"

INFORMATION

This gun is a 9pdr. RML (or MLR) of 8cwt. It is identical to gun no. 3 in the courtyard and probably formed part of the same battery as they have consecutive numbers marked on the breech. The use of steel instead of wrought iron to construct this Armstrong pattern gun might indicate that its date of manufacture was after 1879 when bulk steel production made this type of metal readily available. (Chant. P. 142) The 'omega' shaped supports for the elevating gear are either incorrect or of an early design, later superseded.

MARKS ON GUN

The monogram of Queen Victoria is engraved on top of the jacket and the number 82 is marked on top of the breech. Left trunnion originally marked RGF No. 106? 1874. These marks are now very difficult to make out.

The Council records note that the carriage and wheel hubs of this gun are probably genuine but that the wheels are reproductions. The left wheel hub was originally marked RCD T56653 1886. Although RCD (Royal Carriage Department) is still quite clear the rest of these marks are now virtually illegible (see photo.)

SOUTHSEA CASTLE

Gun No. 26

image ©A.L. Boxell (18.07.2005)

Carronade mounted on rear chock carriage

image ©A.L. Boxell (26.04.2005)

GUN NO. 26	ACCESSION No./ GUN TYPE/CARRIAGE 1967/276 or 1969/297 British Carronade. Rear chock carriage.	LOCATION West Platform

MEASUREMENTS

BARREL Length 33"	CASCABLE dia. 12"	TRUNNION dia. -----	BORE dia. 4¼"

INFORMATION
There is no provenance available for this gun and even the accession number is uncertain. It was probably acquired by the Council in 1967 or 1969. A comprehensive assessment of the carronade can be seen elsewhere in this book. Nicknamed the 'smasher' by the Royal Navy because of its ability to deliver enormous damage to enemy ships at short range, it was no doubt called many other things by those on the receiving end. In common with most carronades this example has no trunnions but is provided with loops underneath. In naval service these would normally be attached to a sliding carriage which recoiled in tandem with the gun. For use on land, where carronades were often used to provide flank defence for coastal defence forts, the rear chock carriage would probably have been seen as a better option than some form of wheeled carriage in order to tame the fierce recoil for which the carronade was notorious.

This recoil, a by product of the reduced windage (see glossary) and relatively light weight of the piece, meant that the carronade never lacked critics, although the gun's proponents were quick to point out that the reduced windage also increased accuracy. A further aspect of the reduction in windage was the increased difficulty experienced in fitting the cannon ball into the muzzle. Consequently later models of the gun were provided with a projecting nozzle at the muzzle end which was scooped internally to allow the loader some 'finger room'.

Just to the rear of the nozzle there is a recess in the muzzle ring, possibly for a removable fore sight, although in this case one would expect to find a raised (permanent) sight on the reinforce ring mid-way down the barrel, in keeping with other carronades of this date.
(cf XIX.236 FT. Nelson)

Behind the breeching loop the button has been threaded to take an elevating screw. The elevating gear is incomplete. On the top surface of the button the two studs were intended to secure a tube which protected the upper end of the screw.

MARKS ON GUN
Just ahead of the vent the weight of the gun (6-0-14) is marked in hundredweights (cwts.) quarters (qrs.) and pounds avoirdupois (lbs.). Further forward still, just behind the reinforce ring, the government broad arrow is very evident. At the side of the barrel some marks show the central axis of the barrel but there is no quarter sight scale marked on the cascable.

On the flat quoin (or coin) patch underneath the cascable the marks '12P Carron 1808 ?203?' can be discerned (with the aid of a mirror) showing that this gun is a 12pounder, made by the Scottish Carron Co. in 1808. Even though the first and last digits of the serial number are illegible in 1808 the first digit would have been a '7'[30], so the serial number of this gun lies between 72030 and 72039.

image ©A.L. Boxell (26.04.2007)

Detail of gun number 26 showing vent, weight of gun in cwts. qrs. and lbs., and the government broad arrow mark.

---

[30] The Carron Co. manufactured a variety of products and this diversity was also evident in their production of ordnance. Although the carronade became their most famous gun the company also cast other types of ordnance and a range of projectiles. Fortunately for historians the company assigned consecutive serial numbers to their guns as they were cast, irrespective of the type or model, and their pieces were marked in a clearly defined manner. For all guns with trunnions the left trunnion bore the serial number, the firm's name and the casting date. For carronades without trunnions similar details can be found on the coin patch underneath the rear of the gun. Serial numbers of guns produced by Carron in 1808 fall between 71820 and 73950 (Watters p. 185)

SOUTHSEA CASTLE

Guns No. 27 and 28
A general view of the West Auxiliary Battery

image ©A.L. Boxell (24.11.2007)

Unfortunately there is no public access to the West Auxiliary Battery as there are safety considerations, the Battery being adjacent to a dry moat of considerable depth. The author takes this opportunity to express his thanks to the management and staff of the castle who provided access to the Battery so that an inspection of the guns could be made

SOUTHSEA CASTLE

Gun No. 27

image ©A.L. Boxell (20.11.2007)

image ©A.L. Boxell (20.11.2007)

GUN NO. 27 On plan	ACCESSION No./ GUN TYPE/CARRIAGE 424/1969 Swedish SBML	LOCATION West Auxiliary Battery

MEASUREMENTS

BARREL Length 11'5"	CASCABLE dia. 23"	TRUNNION dia. 6½"	BORE dia. 7"

INFORMATION

This gun appears to be one of a pair acquired by the Council in 1969.[31] The provenance is very sketchy, being a description of some (partial) marks on gun 27 which are no longer apparent, from which it was deduced that the gun was 'early 18th century'. It seems certain (from the provenance) that it came from Mauritius, so it almost certainly formed part of the fortifications of Port Louis, the capital city.[32]

The gun has a very ugly appearance as the breech end is cut almost square, giving the impression that the barrel has been 'made by the mile and cut off by the yard'. This abrupt termination is not aesthetically pleasing to the eye, nor is it likely to have been very efficient in resisting the explosive force created within the chamber, although the massive base ring probably compensated for any weakness in the design.

Paradoxically the design of the vent is very good. The touch hole and pan are surrounded by an unbroken wall of raised metal some ¼" high in the shape of a cross which would act as a windshield, preventing the gun powder from blowing away before being ignited by the linstock. One disadvantage of this design is that the small reservoir thus created would tend to hold rain or seawater. Presumably this could have been overcome by the use of lead 'aprons' (see glossary) to cover the vent when the gun was not in action.

The button is fairly elongated but is otherwise unremarkable.

---

[31] This is an assumption based on the Council's 'accession numbers'. The other gun of the pair (1969/425) was formerly on the saluting platforms at Southsea but is now allegedly located near the Round Tower, underneath the arches. It has certain features in common with the Castle gun and is also 'from Mauritius'. However, it is listed as a *French 64pdr.*
The gun in the position indicated is most definitely not a 64pdr. nor does it have anything in common with gun 27. Presumably gun 1969/425 has been moved to another location.
[32] Mauritius is an island in the Indian Ocean, situated 530 miles east of Madagascar. The first Europeans to land on the island were the Dutch in 1598, whose occupation was not very persistent as they were chiefly concerned with the exploitation of the ebony forests by convicts. In 1715, after the Dutch left, the deserted island was taken over by the French *Compagnie des Indes (orientales?)* and renamed *Île De France*. Under *Bertrand François Mahé De La Bourdonnais*, governor from 1734, Port Louis was converted into a stone city, strongly fortified.
The Island was occupied by the British during the Napoleonic wars in 1810 and was formally ceded in 1814. Mauritius became independent in March 1968. (New Caxton Encyclopedia)

SOUTHSEA CASTLE

Gun No. 27

image ©A.L. Boxell (20.11.2007)

image ©A.L. Boxell (24.11.2007)

MARKS ON GUN

On the right trunnion the letters VB are cast in relief. These indicate that the founder was Von Berchner which shows that the gun is of Swedish origin. (Brown p. 322). Brown (p.321) makes the point that in the early 18th century the French began producing their own iron guns 'instead of importing Swedish cannon'. As one of these 'imports' of Swedish origin this gun can presumably be dated (very) early 18th century or even late 17th century. Fitting together all the available information, then, it seems probable that this gun was cast in Sweden for the French navy or more likely their East India Co. some time before 1734, after which date it was used to fortify the capital city of Mauritius, St. Louis. Captured by the British in 1810 it would have been brought to England as a war trophy.

The marks on the left trunnion are less distinct than the right but appear to be number 77. There are further numbers on top of the gun which appear to be 66 ^6. On the first reinforce there is a large (royal?) cipher in relief which consists of a crown or coronet surmounting a circular device. The shape of the crown is reminiscent of a British 'naval crown' but no detail is discernible within the circle. Presumably the crown is Swedish.

Portsmouth Council records indicate that the marks N111 and …XV could be found on the gun (in 1969?). These marks are no longer apparent.

image ©A.L. Boxell (20.11.2007)

SOUTHSEA CASTLE

Gun No. 28

image ©A.L. Boxell (20.11.2007)

image ©A.L. Boxell (20.11.2007)

GUN NO. 28 On plan	ACCESSION No./ GUN TYPE/CARRIAGE Accession no. unknown. British SBML	LOCATION West Auxiliary Battery

MEASUREMENTS

BARREL Length 9'	CASCABLE dia. 22"	TRUNNION dia. 6¼"	BORE dia. 6½"

INFORMATION
The second gun comprising the Western Battery is a totally unremarkable Victorian 32pdr. It has a raised vent patch drilled for a flintlock igniter and a pierced button with gate and pin. No weight markings were noticed but the author's inspection of the piece was somewhat hurried because of inclement weather. Unfortunately the West Battery is not open to the general public as there are safety considerations, so any omissions of detail are unlikely to be corrected before publication; a fact for which the author apologises whilst accepting full responsibility.

MARKS ON GUN
Apart from the raised Victorian cipher between the trunnions there appear to be no marks worthy of mention except for some indistinct marks on the left trunnion. These appear to be PO7C (or 6). The gun has no quarter sight marks nor is there a cipher on the chase.

SOUTHSEA CASTLE

Gun No. 29

This naval gun was never adopted by the Royal Navy. It is nonetheless interesting because of the unusual features incorporated in its design.

image ©A.L. Boxell (03.07.2007)

A rifled breech loader, made of steel, with a hexagonal bore, this gun was manufactured at the period of history when the British armed services had all reverted to rifled muzzle loaders made of iron.

image ©A.L. Boxell (03.07.2007)

GUNS 29 and 30	ACCESSION No./ GUN TYPE/CARRIAGE 1967/266 British Whitworth R.B.L.3pdr. Steel 1876	LOCATION Room 1 in Keep

MEASUREMENTS

BARREL Length 40½"	BREECH dia. 10" (approx.)	TRUNNION dia. 3"	BORE dia. 1¾"

INFORMATION

Obtained by the Council in 1967 by courtesy of Lt. Col. Green, who commanded 457 Wessex Regt. Royal Artillery, the two Whitworth guns on display were originally the property of the Isle of Wight battery (T.A.) based at Newport. They are probably the most unusual guns in the castle's collection, having a number of remarkable features seldom seen elsewhere.

The use of steel in their construction in 1876 is itself somewhat remarkable as this date was some five years before this usage became general. The steel construction of Whitworth guns at this early date was made possible by the invention of 'Whitworth steel' which was produced from about 1870. Whitworth's experience had taught him that an unsound gun made of hard steel tended to shatter into pieces thereby endangering the gun crew, whereas an unsound gun made of ductile steel merely became malformed. The use of ductile steel, however, was itself problematical as during its manufacture it could sometimes become honeycombed with air cells which negated its usefulness for the manufacture of guns. Whitworth overcame this difficulty by applying hydraulic pressure to the metal in its fluid state, thus producing a form of mild steel most suitable for gun manufacture.

The fact that these two guns are rifled breech loaders (RBL) made when the British service was using Rifled Muzzle Loaders (RML) is also notable. It is likely, however, that these guns were not made for the British service. Although his guns were never adopted by the British armed forces Whitworth enjoyed considerable sales success elsewhere.[33]

The two guns displayed are virtually identical, but gun 29 has its breech open, while the breech on gun 30 is fully closed. A number of photographs of each gun were taken but as neither gun is complete the reader may experience difficulty in understanding the mechanism. Gun 29 lacks the breech support piece under the breech end but seems otherwise complete. Gun 30 lacks the elevation handle, the rear sight and the loading tray. The two guns are treated as an entity in order to simplify explanation of the mechanism.

---

[33] Whitworth heavy ordnance was sold extensively abroad. Naval guns of his manufacture can be found in Brazil and Denmark, while his small arms were widely used in the home civilian market and in America.

SOUTHSEA CASTLE

Gun No. 29

View of gun showing arrangement of sight

image ©A.L. Boxell (03.07.2007)

These two shells for Whitworth's gun can be seen in the display case in the Keep.

image ©A.L. Boxell (03.07.2007)

The bore is hexagonal and rifled to accept a shell which is also grooved to fit the rifling. Opponents of Whitworth's system claimed that when trialled guns with hexagonal bores were rejected for British military service because the shells tended to jam in the barrel. Alternatively it has been suggested that such jamming occurred because Whitworth failed to manufacture sufficient shells to service his guns on campaign, and consequently gunners were forced to use shells of a type not designed for the gun. The latter argument would hardly explain why Whitworth's guns were rejected by the British trial board, unless the board specifically insisted that all guns tested had to be able to fire all current natures of ammunition. It seems obvious that experience of guns on campaign would only be gained after the guns had been accepted for such service by the trial board. As Whitworth's guns were never accepted for the British service any experience of gun malfunctions on campaign could only have come from their use by foreign services. Presumably this experience would only become apparent over a long period of use so it might be the case that any later malfunctions in the field were used as justification for the prior decision of the British trial board – a case of sentence first, verdict after. Whatever the facts of the matter it seems that adverse government decisions embittered Whitworth to the extent that as he grew older he appeared to become 'increasingly irascible', an attitude no doubt caused by the treatment he received from committees 'whom he regarded as incomparably his inferiors in technical knowledge'. (DNB p. 788)

MARKS ON GUN
Immediately above the breech the barrel is marked with the Whitworth trade mark. The serial number of the gun (1309) surmounts the words 'Joseph Whitworth & Co. Manchester', which form a circle around the words 'trade mark'. The circle also contains an indecipherable incision which presumably is the actual trade mark. Below this circular inscription the date of manufacture (1876) is inscribed, above the word 'Patent'.

CARRIAGE
The cover plate of the elevation mechanism on the rear chock is marked 'WHITWORTH, MANCHESTER'.

SOUTHSEA CASTLE

Gun No. 29

View of gun with breech open. Note that on this gun the breech support piece is missing, consequently the weight of the gun is borne by the breech block, resting on the right cheek of the carriage. The unattached elevating screw can be seen centrally, together with its elevating handle protruding from the rear chock

image ©A.L. Boxell (04.04.2008)

Gun No. 30

The breech support piece correctly attached to the elevating screw. The breech support plate, which would normally take the weight of the rear of the gun, can also be identified

image ©A.L. Boxell (04.04.2008)

SOUTHSEA CASTLE

Guns 29 and 30
Maker's mark on top of breech

image ©A.L. Boxell (04.04.2008)

View underneath gun. Breech support piece on carriage.

image ©A.L. Boxell (04.04.2008)

SOUTHSEA CASTLE

Gun No. 29

This rear view of the gun shows the breech mechanism in the open position. The breech block moves laterally. In the closed position it is strengthened by the series of grooves seen on top of the block. There appears to be a (rifled) loading tray which can be slid forward to carry the shell into the chamber. Although clearly intended for sea service this naval gun was never adopted by the Royal Navy. It is nonetheless interesting because of the unusual features incorporated in its design. A rifled breech loader, made of steel, with a hexagonal bore, the gun was manufactured at the period of history when the British armed services had all reverted to rifled muzzle loaders, made of iron.

The workmanship is of very high quality, as one would expect in anything produced by Whitworth. Critics of his design maintained that the tolerances were too fine as they did not allow for the gunpowder fouling inherent in all black powder guns. This, it was said, would lead to the shell jamming the bore.

image ©A.L. Boxell (07.04.2008)

SOUTHSEA CASTLE

Gun No. 30

This rear view of gun number 30 is included for comparison with gun 29 opposite. The breech is closed. Underneath the gun the breech support piece can just be seen in its correct position, attached to the elevating screw. On this gun, however, there are a few missing parts and the rear sight is broken. The absence of the loading tray will be noted just below what remains of the rear sight, and the elevating handle is also missing.

Although not visible in the photograph, on top of the gun the serial number 1309 can be distinguished just above the inscription Joseph Whitworth & Co., Manchester, together with the date 1876. The gun is not marked with the "crow's foot" so presumably it was never intended for service use, nor are any other proof marks apparent. It has been suggested that the gun was intended for use on a private yacht, although the serial number seems to indicate that too many of these guns were produced for that market.

image ©A.L. Boxell (07.04.2008)

SOUTHSEA CASTLE

Guns 29 and 30
Breech partially closed.

image ©A.L. Boxell (04.04.2008)

Rifled loading tray; seen when breech partially closed.

image ©A.L. Boxell (03.07.2007)

Sir Joseph Whitworth

Joseph Whitworth (1803 – 1887) was born in Stockport. He worked in Manchester and later in London before returning to Manchester at the age of thirty in order to set up his own business manufacturing lathes and machine tools. These products quickly became renowned for their accuracy and workmanship. His innovations included a method of producing accurate flat surfaces and the development of a screw thread which became a British Standard. Another of his inventions, a technique called 'end measurements,' which was demonstrated at the Great Exhibition of 1851, had an accuracy of two millionths of an inch.

In 1859 Whitworth designed a rifle for the British Army which, despite its superiority to the Enfield pattern then in service, was rejected by the War Department as it was prone to fouling. This rejection typified Whitworth's subsequent relationship with the ordnance authorities as although his various gun designs found wide acceptance in the civilian market and were used by foreign armies Whitworth failed to secure their adoption by the British armed forces. Possibly Whitworth's intransigent nature contributed to this failure, but certainly his lack of success led to much public controversy and implications of government bias in favour of the ordnance designs of –

William George Armstrong, 1st Baron Armstrong (1810 – 1900)
Born in Newcastle, Armstrong initially studied Law but switched to engineering. By 1847 he had founded the Elswick works at Newcastle, producing hydraulic machinery, cranes and bridges. After the Crimean War he invented guns of revolutionary design; rifled breech loaders which have always been regarded as marking the birth of modern artillery. In 1859 he was Knighted and was appointed government engineer for rifled ordnance, becoming Superintendent of the RGF at Woolwich. His distaste at the public outcry over government funding of Elswick caused him to resign his government posts, leaving him free to concentrate on the expansion of his business interests. Ironically in 1897 the firms of Armstrong and Whitworth merged and in the first World War the joint firm supplied the British Army with the 18 pounder gun, a weapon which has been described as 'the backbone of the British artillery effort.'

SOUTHSEA CASTLE

Guns No. 31 and 32

Top picture shows mortar in current location at R.E. Museum

image ©A.L. Boxell (05.04.2007)

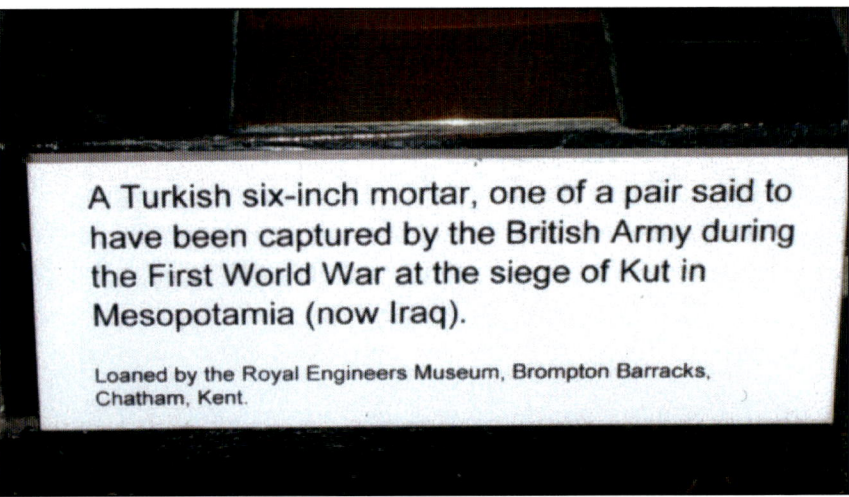

image ©A.L. Boxell (05.04.2007)

GUN NO. 31 & 32	ACCESSION No./ GUN TYPE/ CARRIAGE Loan item. Turkish 6" Brass Mortar	LOCATION On floor in first room of the Keep

MEASUREMENTS

BARREL Length (interior) 9" (13" to bottom of chamber)	CASCABLE dia. 6¾"	TRUNNION dia. 2¾"	BORE dia. 6"

INFORMATION
As shown in photograph of plaque. These mortars are actually the property of the Royal Engineers and are now on display in the introduction area at the R.E. museum. They are included here because at the time of writing they were on loan to Southsea Castle. They are linked historically to Hampshire having been captured by the 115th (Hants. Fortress) Engr., Regt., T.A. This regiment was eventually amalgamated with the 78th Fortress Engineer Regt., which was itself disbanded in 1999.

MARKS ON GUN
Each mortar has a number on the right trunnion, in Arabic, which translate as 1292 and 1294 respectively. The picture below shows the inside of one of the mortars. The vent can easily be identified, as metal polish used to clean the outer surface of the mortar has leaked down the vent into the chamber, leaving the white streaks as shown.

CARRIAGES
The carriages appear to be original. Made of timber, they have a carrying handle at each corner and seem to hold the mortar at a fixed angle of 45°. They measure approximately 32½" long by 8¼" high.

image ©A.L. Boxell (03.07.2007)

SOUTHSEA CASTLE

Gun No. 33

image ©A.L. Boxell (20.11.2007)

image ©A.L. Boxell (20.11.2007)

GUN NO. 33	ACCESSION No./ GUN TYPE/CARRIAGE Accession no. not known. British Royal Mortar	LOCATION Room 2 in Keep

MEASUREMENTS

TOTAL LENGTH 1'4¼"	BODY dia. c. 9"	TRUNNION dia. 2¾"	BORE dia. 5⅝"

INFORMATION

The royal mortar was in land service for over a century with very little change of design. It fired a 16lb. projectile with a maximum range of 1000 yards. Slightly larger than its contemporary (the Coehorn mortar) it outranged it and threw a heavier projectile, but was itself surpassed by the heavier 8" mortar. It could therefore be described as a medium mortar. The Gomer chamber[34] provided good obturation, allowing full advantage to be taken of the propellant force generated by the discharge of the mortar.

The chamber was an improvement on the former cylindrical type as it provided full obturation for the spherical projectile, at least for the initial thrust of the explosion. Hughes (p. 35) states that the 'conical mouth [of the chamber] enabled the projectile to be *rammed* home into it'. (Author's italics) This appears to be a misprint as it is apparent that one of the advantages of a conical chamber is that the ball will fully seat itself in the chamber without being rammed. Any small inconsistencies in ball diameter will be obviated as the ball seats itself in the cone to its requisite depth, after which ramming would serve no purpose.

The first listing of Royal mortars in the Tower of London inventories was in 1726, but the actual date of their invention or the origin of their name is unclear. In 1716 an inventory of arms at Ath, in Belgium, includes 'quartre mortiers de bronze, aux armes de France, nommez mortiers royals, de 6½ pouces de diametre'.[35] This suggests that the name came originally from the French and that Royal mortars were introduced into the English artillery some time between 1716 and 1726. By 1768 the Tower inventory of that year lists them with a calibre of 5.8". Hughes (p. 37) records the calibre as 5½" but the mortars in Southsea Castle are, by actual measurement, 5". If the ammunition varied to the same extent as the Royal mortar calibre seems to have done the Gomer chamber would have been indispensable.

MARKS ON GUN

The date of manufacture on the base ring is rather obscure but appears to be 1822. The weight of the piece (1-1-17) is incised just below the vent and can clearly be seen even in the photograph.

[34] The Gomer chamber was named after its inventor, a Frenchman, Louis-Gabriel de Gomer (1718-98) who was appointed *Inspecteur Général de L'Artillerie* in 1779. The chamber, designed in the form of a truncated cone, the mouth merging smoothly with the bore, was tested in 1785-7 before being incorporated into the Gribeauval system of artillery.

[35] This translates as 'Four bronze mortars, French weapons, called royal mortars, of 6½" diameter'. The French inch (pouce) equalled 27.77mm. so 6½ pouce would be a calibre of 180.5mm or approximately 7"

If the date on the base ring is correct the royal cipher above it should be that of George IV. Unfortunately the cipher is too worn to enable a positive identification to be made.

The carriage is not original. It may have been made up or perhaps it belonged originally to another piece. The Council records state that both their royal mortars originally used a 'hollowed-out block of wood' as a carriage. Presumably these would have been as described in the *'Notes on the Manufactures of the Royal Carriage Department 1868'* (p.52) The bed for the Royal mortar is described as a rectangular block of African Oak or Elm hollowed out sufficiently to receive the breech of the mortar, fitted with cap squares, quoin and rope lifting handles. The dimensions are given as 29" x 13" x 10".

image ©A.L. Boxell (03.07.2007)

Obviously the carriages on which the mortars are now mounted have no need for lifting handles as the rear chock type of carriage is more easily moved on its trucks (wheels). Similarly the elevating gear dispenses with the need for a quoin which has been replaced with a large wooden block designed to take the force of the recoil. The photograph above shows clearly the difference in shape between the Gomer chamber on the 'Royal' mortars and the cylindrical chamber which can be seen on the 'Kut' mortars (guns 31 and 32)

SOUTHSEA CASTLE

Gun No. 34

image ©A.L. Boxell (03.07.2007)

In common with most mortars the trunnions are located at the base of the piece, providing great strength in the chamber area. Although this arrangement allowed the mortar to be adjusted about its base it seems that in the British service the normal practice was to fire the piece at an angle of 45° adjusting the range by varying the charge. This particular mortar is equipped with elevating gear but as emphasised in the text this was not normal.

SOUTHSEA CASTLE

Gun No. 34

image ©A.L. Boxell (20.11.2007)

image ©A.L. Boxell (20.11.2007)

GUN NO. 34 On plan	ACCESSION No./ GUN TYPE/CARRIAGE Accession no. not known. British Royal Mortar.	LOCATION Room 2 in Keep

MEASUREMENTS

BARREL Length 1' 4¼"	BODY dia. c. 9"	TRUNNION dia. 2¾"	BORE dia. 5 ⅝"

INFORMATION

This Royal mortar is virtually identical to gun no. 33 despite the difference in age between them. Their similarity reveals the quality of a design which remained in service for over a century. During this time small variations in calibre and size are recorded but the decision to standardise the calibre of the Royal mortar in the English service has been attributed to the first of the Georgian gun designers, Albert Borgard,[36] an eminent soldier who was by birth a Dane.

The term 'mortar' is said to originate from the weapon's similarity in shape to the domestic mortar in which substances were ground with a pestle. In artillery terms it is used to describe a large calibre weapon designed to fire shells at high angles of elevation. A mortar is the shortest piece of ordnance. It was mainly intended for siege warfare and it was 'considered to be ideal for attacking a town since [it] could lob a hollow gunpowder-packed projectile over the walls.'(Henry p. 11) In the British service it was usually fired at 45°, the range being altered by adjusting the charge weight. Its use was not of course limited to siege warfare, as its high trajectory meant that the 'bomb' carried over enemy field defences, enabling it to engage targets that were sheltered from normal artillery fire. As early as 1850 mortars could also be used to fire parachute 'light balls'[37] which could be used to light the battlefield at night, and smoke balls to obscure friendly troop movements by day.[38]

---

[36] According to Caruana (Smith p. 12) Borgard was the first man to design a complete system of artillery. Apparently the various guns within his system were not named (in accordance with previous practice) but were described by their calibre. Confusingly, however, Caruana states that '[Borgard] disposed of the nominal terminology in guns and he probably introduced the Royal calibre.' This apparent contradiction seems to indicate that Borgard kept the name 'Royal' for these mortars, but laid down regulations governing their calibre.Initially guns were categorised by name (Saker, Minion, etc) and the transition into their categorisation by calibre is also confusing. Munday (p.12) gives a believable account of the origin of this process, stating that captured enemy guns, when pressed into British service, had calibres not found in the British arsenal and consequently such guns were described by their calibre. This occurred from the second half of the 17th century. It seems likely, therefore, that (circa) 1714 when Borgard designed his new system of artillery he would have taken the opportunity to clarify what would, by then, have become an unsatisfactory descriptive muddle.By ending the nominal terminology he would, of course, not only have introduced order into the system in use at the time but also have avoided subsequent problems of a descriptive nature.

[37] The first parachute jump was made in 1783. A Frenchman, Sébastien Lenormand, jumped from a tower at Montpellier. He used a conical canopy which probably explains the shape of the parachute supporting the 'light ball' (see drawing)

SOUTHSEA CASTLE

Guns No. 33 and 34. Royal Mortars.

This drawing of a 'parachute' light ball was taken from the Royal Laboratory plates, 1850. It would nowadays be known as a 'flare' but its function is still the same, to light up the battlefield at night and reveal enemy troop movements. On occasion smoke bombs would also be fired from mortars to obscure the movements of our own troops when forming up for an attack, or at any time when cover from view was considered essential.

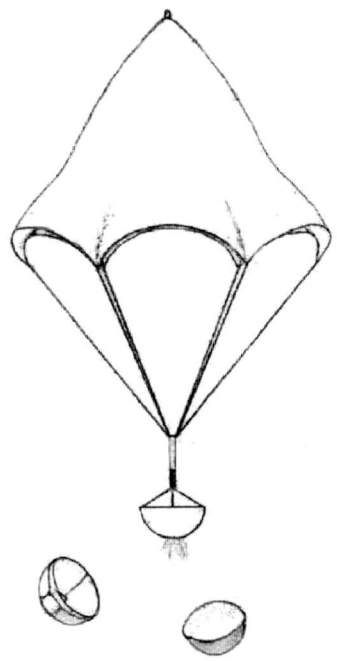

[38] Mortars offered scope for initiatives also. At the great siege of Gibraltar in 1779 an infantry officer, Captain Mercier of the 39th Regt., suggested firing the 5½" shell of the Royal mortar with short fuzes from 24pdr. cannons, which had a similar calibre. The increased range of the mortar bombs thus obtained allowed the defenders to engage enemy working parties with airburst projectiles. After the siege the idea was taken further by a Lt. Shrapnel, who in 1784 developed the shell named after him.

MARKS ON GUN

On the main body of the piece the royal cipher of George III is quite clear. Just below the base ring but above the vent the makers name and date are given as I & H King 1807, which identifies the mortar as a product of the R.B.F (See 'Royal Brass Foundry'). Just below the vent the weight of the piece is shown as 1-1-15, making it two pounds lighter than its twin, gun no. 33.

Like its companion also, the carriage is either a reproduction or has been obtained from elsewhere, as the Royal mortars were not usually equipped with elevating gear.

It would be inappropriate to close this description of the Royal mortar without further comment on the designer attributed with standardising its calibre in the English service.

Albert Borgard (1659-1751) was a most remarkable soldier. In 1688 he left the Danish army and fled abroad for reasons which remain obscure, although a contemporary Danish document mentions that he had been implicated in a treasonable matter. He spent some years as a mercenary soldier for various armies (Polish, Prussian, French) before joining the English artillery. He was then aged only 33, but is described as one of the 'most experienced artillery and engineer officers in the world.' (DNB. P. 658) In the English service he saw action in Flanders, Spain, Portugal and Minorca. At Villa Viciosa he was wounded, left for dead and taken prisoner but was later exchanged, on his return to England becoming chief firemaster on 9th August 1712. He was amongst the injured at the Moorfields explosion (see 'Royal Brass Foundry') but survived to become eventually the assistant surveyor of the ordnance. His planning in that post led to the formation of the Royal Artillery, a regiment of which he became the first Colonel in 1722, and which survives today as his enduring legacy.

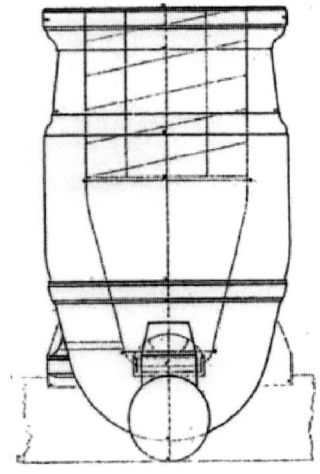

SOUTHSEA CASTLE

Guns No. 35 and 36

Gun 35

image ©A.L. Boxell (05.04.2007)

image ©A.L. Boxell (05.04.2007)

GUN NO. 35/36	ACCESSION No./ GUN TYPE/CARRIAGE Accession no. not known. British Carronade	LOCATION Room 3 in Keep

MEASUREMENTS

BARREL Length 29½"	CASCABLE dia. 6¼"	TRUNNION dia. 2"	BORE dia. 2¼"

INFORMATION

These two carronades are unusual for a variety of reasons but as there is no difference whatsoever between them they are being considered as a pair, rather than individually. They are extremely small, the calibre being probably 1lb. or 2lbs. The Blomefield loop at the rear dates them after 1787, when the loop was introduced, and they have a vent patch, drilled for the attachment of a flintlock igniter. The nozzle at the muzzle dates from 'early 1790s' (Watters p. 173). The most unusual features are their trunnions as carronades, unlike other cannon, were usually equipped instead with a loop underneath the gun by which they were attached to the carriage.

MARKS ON GUNS

The guns have no discernible marks of any kind. However, the mere absence of marks provides information in itself. The Carron Co. who designed the carronade were quite meticulous in marking their guns so the absence of marks indicates that these guns were made elsewhere. It is known that, for example, the Falkirk Iron Co. made small carronades for merchant ships from about 1800. (Watters p. 173) These two carronades are certainly small and the absence of the government 'crows-foot' mark means that they must have been intended for use on merchant ships, or perhaps on an armed yacht.

PART TWO

CARRONADES

Introduced by the Carron company of Falkirk in 1778, carronades were 'designed to fire the largest possible shot in terms of [their] own weight at low velocities'. (Guilmartin p.84). They used a powder charge one third or one quarter of that used by a normal cannon for the same weight projectile and the carronade itself weighed about a quarter of a normal gun of similar calibre. The terminal ballistics were good, as it had been found that the optimum damage to an enemy ship was inflicted when a ball of reduced velocity was used. This tended to produce wooden splinters, whereas a higher velocity ball tended to hole the hull of a ship, passing right through without creating any splinters, thus reducing casualties among the enemy crew from these secondary missiles. The carronade was invented by Gen. Robert Melville and Charles Gascoigne (gunfounder and a partner of the company). Officially introduced into the Navy in 1779 it proved to be a mixed blessing and became obsolete circa 1870.

Although this weapon had a long service life, much of it in the merchant service where it was particularly popular, it was never short of naval detractors. Possibly its supporters were influenced by its undoubted financial advantages. Its economical use of gunpowder was one obvious saving, while its smaller gun crew resulted in less obvious but no less important savings in terms of pay, victualling and living space. It produced good terminal ballistics at short range, its reduced windage gave it greater accuracy while its short barrel facilitated reloading. Its close range destructive power allied to the financial aspect would explain its popularity with officials who nowadays would probably summarise its capabilities as providing 'more bang for your buck'

Unfortunately the 'bang' from a short barrelled, light-weight weapon led inevitably to greater recoil and muzzle flash. These characteristics meant that the front of the gun, barely protruding from the gun port, could ignite rigging and/or the hammock barricade while at the rear of the piece care had to be taken to ensure that in recoiling the 'vertical connecting bolt' linking the upper and lower parts of the sliding carriage did not contact the rear end of the travelling slot. If badly set up or, more worryingly, if the breeching rope stretched too much in action, the bolt could be broken, putting the piece out of action. In addition to this self destructive possibility the carronade's sliding carriage was more vulnerable to enemy fire than the normal truck carriage. The greater accuracy of the carronade, emanating from its reduced windage, was negated by its lack of range while its ability to deliver a greater 'punch' at short range than normal cannons was compromised by the fact that, unlike them, because of its already fearsome recoil it could not be double shotted. Consequently, although lauded as a short range 'smasher', it is doubtful if its actual ability exceeded that of a normal cannon in a ripple broadside when passing or raking an enemy ship, when normal cannons could be double shotted, slowing their muzzle velocity and allowing the additional use of case shot. Only in a long term broadside 'slogging match' would its reputation be justified, when its shorter reloading time and repeated ability to deliver a heavier 'punch' could be used to full advantage.

The experience of the Lake Erie squadron in the war against America (1775-1781) showed that ships armed solely with carronades could be at a tactical disadvantage when exposed to long range enemy fire, consequently the carronade could never replace the main armament but would always be relegated to a secondary role. Ultimately, the carronade has to be judged on whether its adoption as a service weapon marked a significant advance to the Navy's ability to wage war. Judging by this criterion leads to the inevitable conclusion that, on balance, the weapon had only a limited significance.

image ©A.L. Boxell (26.04.2007)

image ©A.L. Boxell (26.04.2007)

ROYAL BRASS FOUNDRY

In 1684 a Maximilian Western established a gun foundry at Moorfields in London, nearly opposite the present headquarters of the Honourable Artillery Company. In 1704 the foundry was leased to Matthew Bagley, a former bell founder of Chalcombe, Northampton, who took over the government gun contracts still outstanding. In 1706 Bagley was formally appointed Founder to the Office of Ordnance. In that capacity he became responsible for the supply of all the Ordnance Board's brass requirements, from small arms parts to cannon.

On 10th May 1716 a horrific accident at the Moorfields Foundry changed the attitude of government towards armaments manufacture in Britain. The accident, attributed to pouring molten gun metal into a damp mould, killed Bagley and some sixteen others and persuaded the Board of Ordnance to set up a government run foundry where safety could be better controlled. With commendable speed the Royal Brass Foundry, designed by Sir John Vanbrugh, was completed in 1717 and a Swiss national, Andrew Schalch, was employed as Master Founder, a post he held for 54 years.

Eventually in 1770 (with some difficulty due to his irascibility) he was replaced by two Dutchmen, Jan and Peter Verbruggen, who modernised production by introducing solid casting together with the use of the horizontal boring machine.[39] After the death of Peter Verbruggen in 1786 the post of Master Founder was abolished until 1797.

As it was customary to put the name of the founder on brass guns, knowledge of the senior management at the RBF will prove helpful in dating these pieces.

John and Henry King, two Scots, had been employed as founders in the RBF since 1784 becoming foreman and assistant foreman in 1789. They became respectively Master Founder and Assistant Founder on the revival of these offices in 1797. John King continued as Master Founder until his death in 1813, being succeeded in that post by his brother Henry.

Cornelius King, the son of John, had been foreman since 1805. On the death of his father in 1813 he was promoted to Assistant Founder, his place as foreman being taken by William North. When Henry King retired in 1818 the post of Master Founder was again abolished. Cornelius was then left in charge of RBF with the rank of Assistant Founder. He retired in

---

[39] Solid Casting: This technique relied on the use of a horizontal boring lathe invented by Johann Maritz in 1714. This machine meant that for the first time gun barrels could be cast in solid form, the bore being drilled out after casting. Formerly the barrel had been cast around a core, the resulting bore being lightly skimmed. This meant that the bore was often slightly out of line with the central axis of the gun and sometimes had dangerous imperfections.

Maritz's lathe was so designed that the outside of the barrel could be turned simultaneously with the drilling of the bore, allowing faster production of a more accurate gun. It is recorded (Ffoulkes p.68) that Schalch never commenced casting without holding group prayers beforehand, prompting my thought that the accuracy of his guns depended as much on prayer as on the expertise of his foundry workers.

1822 and William North then moved up to Assistant Founder. North must have kept that post until at least 1849 as his name is shown on the base ring of gun No. 9, but subsequently (c.1853) his place was taken by Samuel Eccles, originally a Modeller, who retired in 1855.

After 1771 the Royal Brass Foundry was able to meet all the requirements of the Ordnance Board, so the system of contracting out some of the work ceased. Consequently all brass ordnance *in the British Service* after that date should bear one of the names below, and the name will give a broad indication of the casting date. Of course private foundries continued to bid for contracts for other customers, such as the East India Co., and the RBF also made cannon for other customers, usually as presentation pieces for political reasons. The names below therefore indicate the foundry of origin (RBF) but do not necessarily mean that the gun bearing the name was employed in the British service.

NAME ON GUN	DATE OF CASTING
A. Schalch	1717 – 1771
J & P Verbruggen	1771 – 1786
J (or I) and H. King	1786 – 1818
C. King	1818 – 1822
W. North	1822 – 1849
S. Eccles	c 1853 - 1855

GUN METALS. BRASS, BRONZE AND IRON

For convenience, the gun metals used in the construction of cannon can be divided into 'brass and 'iron', but these convenient labels actually over-simplify the matter. Guns made from iron, for example, were initially made from wrought iron which suited the type of technology then employed in gun construction.

Although iron guns had been cast on the Continent for some time the requisite technology was unknown in England until (circa) 1543, when Henry VIII employed two Dutchmen to instruct English artisans in the procedure. Readers need not concern themselves with wrought iron guns made before 1543 as these pieces, being far too valuable to be exposed to the elements, are nowadays found only in museums. Essentially, then, any iron gun mentioned herein can be assumed to be made of cast iron unless indications are given to the contrary.

Prior to 1543 'brass' guns had been cast for many years both in England and abroad, as the properties of this type of gun metal lent themselves more readily to the casting process. After the advent of cast iron guns in 1543 brass guns continued to be manufactured despite the savings in cost offered by the use of cast iron. This was because although brass guns were expensive and tended to heat up after prolonged use, a situation which could lead to barrel droop,[40] they had the advantage of being lighter and therefore easier to handle than iron guns. In general they were not very successful when employed either for coastal defence or siege operations (Henry. (b) p.5) although they were of course well suited for use as horse drawn field guns. After the first siege of Badajoz (1811) Major-Gen Sir Alexander Dickson, in a letter to Gen. McLeod, wrote "I think 17 or 18 24pounders were rendered *hors de combat"* (Henry (b) p.36) He went on to note that only two of these were caused by enemy fire. The rest were the result of 'drooping at the muzzle and unbushing'[41] In a letter to Admiral Berkeley before the second siege of Badajoz, in 1812, Wellington complained that he had "had enough of sieges with defective artillery", and pointed out that he had repeatedly requested guns and shot of "Carron manufacture".[42] (Watters p.181). Whether he ever received these iron guns as replacements for the brass ones used in 1811 is not recorded, although the successful conclusion to the 1812 siege might indicate that he did. The term 'brass', when used as a designation for a type of cannon, requires explanation. Four metals (copper, tin, zinc and lead) can be found in gun metal alloys. Blackmore (p.408) points out that "Any copper alloy used in making guns in the 15th to the 18th centuries which was composed of 2,3 or 4 of these metals was generally referred to as 'brass". In modern times the word brass has come to mean an alloy of copper and zinc while bronze is now used to distinguish the alloy of copper and tin. Throughout this book the traditional term brass has been retained in this context irrespective of the actual composition of the alloy.

[40] 'Barrel droop' was a phenomenon caused by overheating of the barrel which, as the name implies, caused it to curve downwards, affecting the gun's accuracy and endangering the gun crew.
[41] 'Unbushing'. When the cannon fired a considerable amount of gas escaped through the vent, gradually burning away the metal until the enlarged vent became unserviceable. This problem was resolved by 'bouching' the vent preferably with a copper insert. When the insert itself became too large, or was blown out of the gun by the backblast, the gun was said to be 'unbushed'
[42] The Carron Company was a Scottish ironworks established in 1759 on the North bank of the river Carron near Falkirk in Stirlingshire. After initial problems with cannon production the company grew to become the largest iron works in Europe.

IGNITION SYSTEMS FOR GUNPOWDER

THE LINSTOCK

There appear to have been various forms of linstock although no doubt from time to time there must have been some form of standard issue. Some still in existence have rather obviously been made by the gunner himself; these would no doubt have been employed on merchant ships. Some types of linstocks had a point on the base so that they could be stuck in the ground or into the deck of a ship. The details shown in the photograph seem to be authentic, right down to the powder smudges on the gunner's cheeks (and the apprehensive look on his face.) The end of the slow match is held rigidly in position by two wing nuts which allow it to be rapidly advanced in order to maintain the glowing end in the optimum position to effect ignition of the cannon. The surplus part of the match has been wrapped around the shaft which not only stores it conveniently but also provides a better grip for the gunner, while the length of the shaft allows the gunner to keep clear of the gun's recoil. This particular linstock can be seen in action in the section of the book entitled '*Bushing the Vent*'.

Photo taken at Fort Nelson and shown by kind permission
of Board of Trustees of Royal Armouries

IGNITION SYSTEMS FOR GUNPOWDER

Most people are aware that a projectile is propelled from a cannon by the explosive force generated by gunpowder, but far fewer people could explain the mechanics of the process, except to state that when gunpowder is lit, it explodes. This of course is true, but it hardly suffices as an adequate explanation of the forces unleashed when a cannon is fired; a process initiated by an ignition system. Before describing the various ignition systems employed during the gunpowder era it is advantageous to know something about gunpowder itself, as although the igniter may vary the reaction of the gunpowder, when lit, is always the same. So, what are the properties of this harmless looking powder which has such explosive potential?

The most notable characteristic is that it is not really a powder at all. It is really a granular mixture – the granules being graded to suit usage. Fine powder would burn more quickly than coarse powder. For some uses, such as a propellant used in small arms the granules would be very fine, but again for some modern uses the granules could be one inch diameter cubes. Whatever their size, though, the granules were composed of three constituents, saltpetre, (potassium nitrate) charcoal and sulphur which long experience showed were best mixed in the proportion 75% 15% and 10%. When lit the powder *burns* and turns into gas,[43] creating a volume of gas 500 times larger than its original volume, which under the expansive action of the liberated heat rises to 4000 times its own volume. This burning occurs at a speed of approximately one quarter mile per second (900 mph). When confined (as in the chamber of a cannon, for instance) it creates enormous pressure which has to escape its confinement. In doing so it will always follow the line of least resistance, so the only moveable part of its containment, the projectile, is expelled from the barrel with great force. As the pressure operates in all directions the gun is forced backwards in a movement known as recoil, but because the weight of the gun is so much greater than the projectile its movement is slower, and therefore controllable to some extent.

This whole process had to be initiated by ignition of the gunpowder which, as it was contained within the cannon, was not a simple matter and various forms of igniter have been devised to effect it. The main problem with which gunners had to contend was the speed of ignition which particularly for naval guns, resting as they did on an unstable firing platform, should be as nearly instantaneous as possible. The slightest delay between the gunner's decision to fire and the actual discharge of the piece meant that the ship's movement had altered the point of aim. A similar problem could be encountered by field artillery when engaging crossing targets but for land based guns the difficulties would be less acute and less frequently met. Siege guns, for example, might never be called upon to engage a moving target. This probably explains why the army lagged so far behind the Navy in the adoption of the flintlocks....continued on page 128.

---

[43] Gunpowder is classified as a low explosive (nowadays called a propellant) which accomplishes its effect by *burning*. Its action is markedly different from a high explosive (H.E.) which *detonates*. Gunpowder turns into gas as it burns progressively, in parallel layers, from the outside inwards, each granule igniting those next to it (Piobert's law). When detonated a high explosive also becomes gas, but through a chemical reaction which causes an almost instantaneous rearrangement of its molecular structure. The 'detonating wave' travels at approximately 6miles per second, producing a high 'brisance' or shattering effect. In simple terms H.E. provides a punch, whereas a low explosive is more like a push.

IGNITION SYSTEMS FOR GUNPOWDER

Photo taken at Fort Nelson and shown by kind permission of
Board of Trustees of Royal Armouries

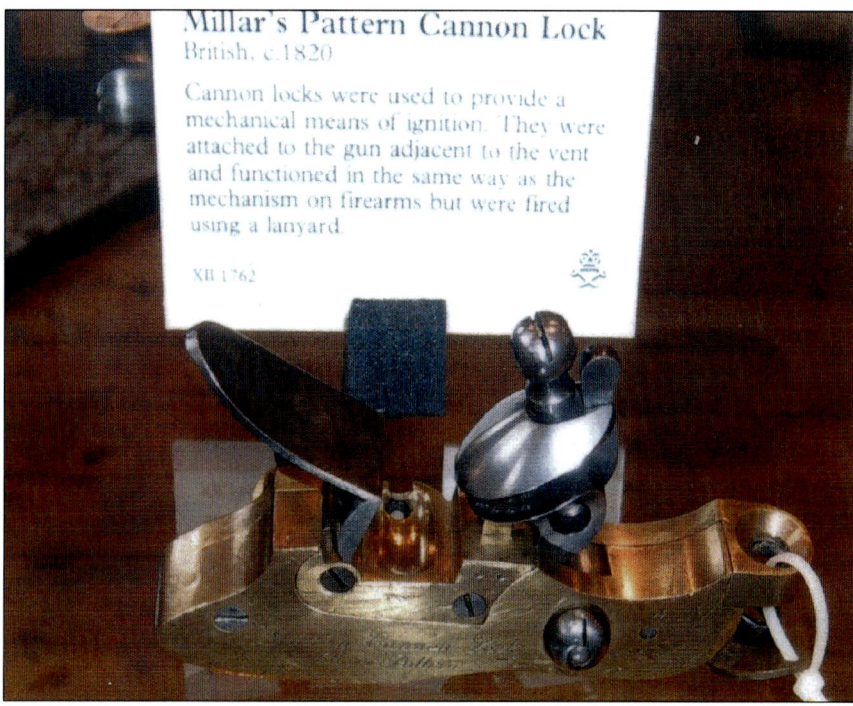

image ©A.L. Boxell (25.07.2005)

Cannon locks were used to provide a mechanical means of ignition. They were attached to the gun adjacent to the vent and functioned in the same way as the mechanism on firearms, but were fired using a lanyard. XII, 1762.

For a long time the Royal Navy was reluctant to use flintlocks with tin primer tubes as in the confines of a gun deck the tube, which was forcibly ejected from the vent when the gun was fired, constituted a hazard to the gun crews. In 1755 Admiral Anson published an order authorizing the issue of flintlocks and tin primer tubes to 'all his Majesty's ships now... or hereafter fitting or refitting for sea.' These items were intended to be used only on the quarterdecks where the tubes would present less danger to the crew, but there seems to be no evidence that ship's Captains complied with the order. After Sir Charles Douglas's invention, the quill primer tube, proved its value at the Battle of the Saints, however, flintlocks and their accessories became standard issue in the Navy.

Continued from page 126... For several centuries before the flintlock came into service as an ordnance igniter, though, the method of ignition for cannon was the linstock. Although these were often of fanciful design they were essentially a stick to which was attached a length of slow match. The match was a length of rope soaked in saltpetre so that once lit it smouldered for a long time, providing a continual source of ignition. The linstock was about a yard long, allowing the firer to stand aside from the recoil of the gun which resulted from his 'touching off' the ignition train.[44] This procedure did not lack danger to the gun crew nor was it particularly efficient. The loose powder constituted a continual hazard and on naval gun decks the gun captain responsible for laying (aiming) the piece could not operate the linstock as he carried the powder horn round his neck, consequently there would always be a delay between the gun captain's order to fire and its implementation by the linstock operator, leading to the loss of accuracy already described.

In the mid 1700's most of the disadvantages of the system were resolved, in the land service, by the invention and speedy introduction of the 'quick match tube'. Quick match consisted of a cord which was permeated with saltpetre then rolled in fine gunpowder before being dried. When ignited it burnt very rapidly and short lengths of it were enclosed in a tin tube which could be inserted in the touch hole of the cannon. When set off by the slow match it transferred the flash instantaneously down the tube to ignite the charge. This immediately averted the dangers emanating from the previous system of priming the vent with loose gunpowder but the tin tube provided its own hazards, as it was ejected from the gun by the back pressure up the vent when the gun fired. Although it would have been possible to construct guns for land service with the touch hole angled so that the tube would be ejected safely forward, in the confines of a naval gun deck the tube would always present a hazard, both as a missile which would ricochet from the deck above on ejection and subsequently, when its presence rolling around the deck provided a constant danger to the bare feet of the naval gunners. For this reason the Admiralty refused to adopt the system for some time.

The use of the flintlock, combined with the quick match tube, would appear to be a natural progression although there seems to be no evidence that the Artillery adopted this form of ignition until they made them general issue 'well into the 1830s' (Wilkinson-Latham p.40). In this matter they lagged well behind the Navy which was itself somewhat tardy in its adoption. In 1755 Anson had advocated the use of flintlocks, together with tin primer tubes, for firing cannons, but only for ordnance situated on the quarter-deck (PRO ADM 2/225). Presumably this was because on an open deck with no overhead obstruction the ejection of the primer tube would no longer present a hazard... continued on page 130.

---

[44] The ignition train was a continual train of gunpowder leading from the touch hole down the vent until it contacted the main charge, which was contained within a cartridge made of paper or cloth. Once the cartridge was inserted from the muzzle of the gun and had been rammed into place in the chamber a pricker was inserted down the vent to open up the cartridge bag. A powder horn carried by the gunner was then used to fill up the vent with fine (pistol) powder which was then 'touched off' by the linstock.

IGNITION SYSTEMS FOR GUNPOWDER

Improved 'double-headed' flintlock invented in 1817 by Howard Douglas. If one flint broke in action a replacement could be utilised by turning the flints through 180 degrees

Fort Nelson lock shown by kind permission of Board of Trustees of Royal Armouries

Opposite side of Douglas's flintlock showing channel by which sparks were directed on to the head of the quill tube. The wing nut used to turn the flints can also be clearly seen

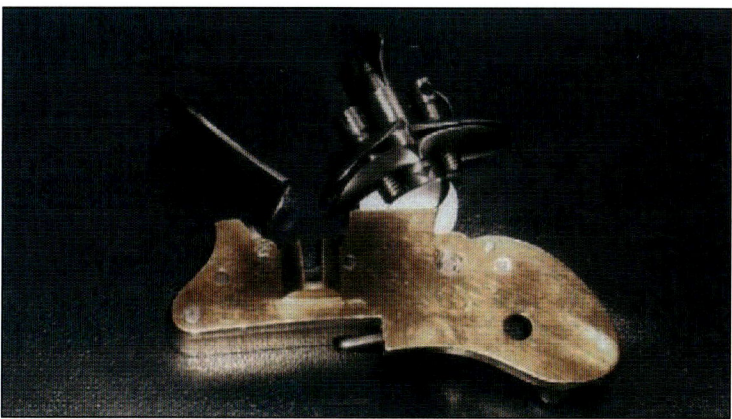

Cont from p 128...The vent could have been angled to eject the tube overboard, but there is no evidence that this was ever done, nor does there seem to be any evidence that this Admiralty order of 21:10:1755 was ever put into effect (Munday p.13). Although the order specified that 'all his Majesties ships now... or hereafter fitting or refitting for sea [are] to be fitted with locks... and a sufficient number of tin tubes for priming them.' no specific mention was made of these items when HMS *Captain* refitted on 08:11:1755 (ADM2/263) nor were they mentioned when *Dreadnought* refitted some time later. (ADM2/266).

In fact, according to Hogg (p.31) there 'does not seem to have been any attempt to fit [flint locks] to a gun vent until 1778, when Sir Charles Douglas urged [their use] on the Admiralty'. 1778 was the year in which Capt. Douglas took command of the *Duke,* a 98 gun ship of the line. On his appointment to that position he 'brought before the Admiralty and the Ordnance several propositions for improving, facilitating and quickening the service of the naval ordnance'. (Douglas p. 398). These consisted of the introduction of flannel to replace the paper which was being used to make cartridges, as flannel was less likely to leave any smouldering residue in the bore which would need removal with a 'wormhook'. He repeatedly urged that his ship be equipped with flintlocks 'by which the use of the slow match and powder horn for priming might more or less be discontinued' (Douglas p. 398) but his most innovative and, as events proved, his most important suggestion was that the tin priming tubes should be replaced by 'quill tubes' made from goose feathers. At that time quill pens were used for writing and it is most probable that Douglas realised how these everyday implements could be used to suit this purpose. The central stem of the goose feather was hollow and it could therefore be packed with an explosive composition. On firing the whole quill would be consumed by the ignition flash, thus eliminating the missile hazard inherent in the use of tin tubes and removing the obstacle in the path of the introduction of flint locks to serve the 'great guns'. When the Admiralty, with its customary caution, supplied the *Duke* with a total of only eight locks (Douglas p. 398) Sir Charles took matters into his own hands and outfitted his ship at his own expense (see expense account). At first quills of different lengths were used, depending on the calibre of the gun, as it was assumed that the quill was required almost to touch the charge in order to ignite it. Later, however, experience showed that a quill length of 2½" would produce a lance of flame some 6" long, so quill tubes were standardised at 2½". The importance of their invention can hardly be overstated, as their impact upon naval gunnery was profound. The flannel cartridge, too, was singularly important for safety reasons as it avoided 'the danger of pieces of paper cartridge lurking in the gun, or flickering about like touch paper between decks, being brought in by the wind after the gun was fired, or by indraughts of air through the ports'. (Douglas p. 285) In fact the flintlock completely removed the need to prime the gun with loose powder. Reference to the illustrations of the Naval flintlocks shows that the shower of sparks from the frizzen would be cascaded into a channel which directed them down and to one side of the lock, where they would ignite the head of the quill tube. This is confirmed by Gascoigne's letter of 17th May 1782 touting his carronade to a prospective customer in which the inventor states that because of certain features of the gun '... you cannot use priming powder, but have to apply a quick match instead which has been found to be reliable on every occasion.' After noting that by 'using both the flanel [sic] cartridges and the match you prevent spilling powder on the deck as well as the burning out of the vent when the gun is fired' he concludes by mentioning that he proposes to extend the use of hand locks which 'feature an aperture in their bottom which is placed on the quick match and the gun can be fired while aiming it.' (Smith p. 33)

In summary, then, the improvements resulting from Capt. Douglas's innovations were the avoidance of danger to the gunners from the spillage of loose gunpowder; the lessened risk of premature ignition of the charge from smouldering cartridge paper and less need to use the wormhook to remove cartridge remnants, giving faster reloading time; the removal of hazards arising from the use of tin tubes; increased speed of ignition of the gun, leading to greater accuracy and transferring the action of firing via the lock to the gun captain so that he no longer had to rely on subordinates for the shot release. A further advantage was that it was also possible for quill tubes to be made on board and, once the standard size of 2½" was introduced it was possible to issue a standard kit for making the tubes to all ships of the fleet.

The Navy's debt to the Douglas family was increased when, in 1817, Sir Charles's son Howard invented an improved flintlock. This carried a double flint so that if one flint broke in action the flint head could be quickly turned through 180° to utilise the second (see illustration, page 129).

The advantages of the new ignition system soon became apparent and by 1790 the fleet had been outfitted with brass locks. Some older cannon had to be adapted to take locks but in 1787 Blomefield's new design of gun was cast with a vent 'patch' on top to which gun locks could be attached. The flintlock system lasted for many years but was eventually superseded in the Navy in 1831 by the rather similar percussion lock, which the Army also adopted in 1845. (Hogg & Batchelor, p.36.) The percussion principle relied for its effect on a mixture of potassium chlorate and fulminate of mercury which was sensitive to shock. The mixture was placed in a small copper cap which, when struck by the gun's hammer, exploded, sending a flash down the vent to ignite the main charge. Its operation was quicker than the flintlock and small-arms could be converted to the new system which ensured its popularity. By 1845 the new system had virtually replaced the flintlock.

The final ignition system which needs description here is the friction tube. This was a method which was used solely for ordnance and to some extent was a retrogression in that it was initially used with the quill tube by the Navy but reverted to the use of a copper tube by the Army. Dropped into the vent of the gun it was fired by a lanyard which dragged a roughened piece of metal through the phosphorus topping, (see photo.) much like the ignition of the domestic match.

Subsequently more sophisticated methods of ignition were developed but these were employed in guns of more modern design than those described in this book. Throughout the 19th century chemists had constantly tried to find a replacement for gunpowder. This was effected for small arms by 1886 when Vielle of France perfected the first reliable smokeless propellant, but for major ordnance gunpowder was the only satisfactory propellant until 1891 when Abel and Dewar perfected a compound of nitro-cellulose, nitro-glycerine and mineral jelly (Vaseline) which, being extruded into thin cords, became known as 'Cordite'.

This new propellant "enabled smokeless charges to produce as much velocity as gunpowder without exceeding the safe chamber pressure." (Hogg & Batchelor p. 101).

Consequently gunpowder was no longer used as a propellant and the gunpowder era was virtually at an end. It was still used for blasting and other purposes but its need for a speedy ignition system no longer existed.

EXPENSE ACCOUNT

Extract from *A Treatise on Naval Gunnery* 1855

Some of the expenses incurred by Captain Charles Douglas in outfitting H.M.S. *Duke* with flintlocks. As the *Duke* was a second rate she would have carried at least 98 guns, so some estimate of the total cost to her Captain is apparent in the account shown below.

"AN ACCOUNT of Expenses by me incurred for the better use of the Cannon of H. M. S. the 'Duke,' under my command, between the beginning of the year 1780 and the day of the date hereof.

	£	s.	d.
To 28 left-hand locks¹ at 10s. 6d., made by Mr. Sandwell, of Tower-hill, gunsmith	14	14	0
To 400 best black flints at 2s. 6d. per hundred . .	0	10	0
To carriage and porterage of said locks and flints from London	0	2	6
To 1004 goose-quills for tubes	3	9	4
To spirits of wine to make an inflammable paste for the tops thereof, to keep in the powder	0	15	6
To sewing silk for tying down and crossing their heads to keep in such paste	0	12	6
To 71 yards of flannel at 1s. 2d. per yard, for bottoms to paper cartridges	4	2	10
To worsted for sewing in ditto	1	4	6
	25	11	2

Given under my hand, on board H. M. S. 'Duke,' at sea, the 13th March, 1781,

(Signed) CHARLES DOUGLAS."

" These are to certify that the foregoing articles are actually in use on board this His Majesty's Ship in my department, in quantity and quality as above-mentioned; and I do moreover certify, to the best of my knowledge and belief (I myself having purchased sundry of the said articles for Sir Charles Douglas), that the charges of the whole thereof are fairly stated.

Witness my hand, on board H. M. S. 'Duke,' at sea, 13th March, 1781,

(Signed) WM. IRELAND."

IGNITION SYSTEMS FOR GUNPOWDER

FRICTION TUBE

The final system described in the text for the ignition of gunpowder was the friction tube. This differed slightly from the flintlock system in that, being inappropriate for use in small arms, it could only be used for ordnance. The vertical section consisted of a copper tube containing 9grams of fine pistol powder held in place by a small cork. This part of the igniter was inserted into the touch hole. The horizontal arm (see illustration) contained phosphorous which was ignited by dragging a piece of roughened metal through it, much like the operation of the domestic match head. This then ignited the powder contained within the vertical section which in turn set off the main charge. The ring on the end of the horizontal arm was for the attachment of a lanyard. As the pull on the lanyard would need to be in line with the horizontal arm of the igniter a lanyard guide would usually be screwed into the gun near the vent. The holes for these guides can be seen on some guns but the guides themselves are usually missing.

Correctly designated 'TUBE FRICTION COPPER SOLID DRAWN mark 2 (L)' the igniter obviously underwent a number of modifications. Unfortunately no examples of these igniters seem to exist but the reproduction shown in the illustration indicates their method of operation.[45] A more detailed drawing can be found in PRO SUPPLY 5/43.

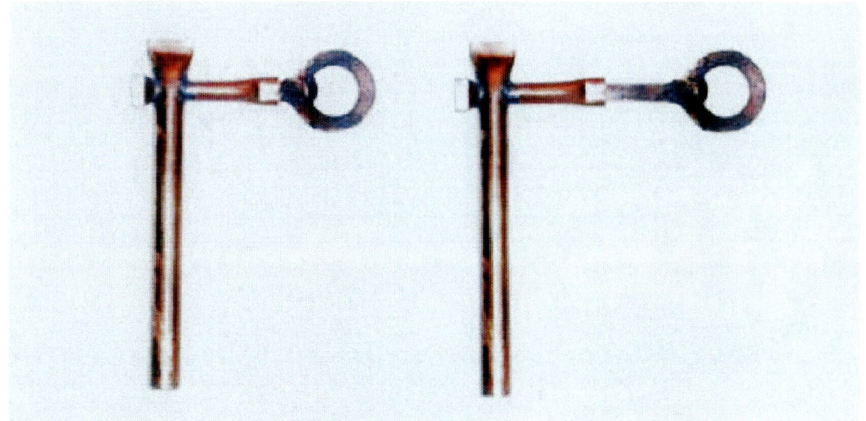

---

[45] For the reproduction of the igniter tube I am indebted to Mr. J. Sadler, Fort Nelson.

GLOSSARY

Apron. A Shaped lead cover used to protect the vent and igniter mechanism on ship's guns, and keep them dry.

Astragal. Small, convex, half-round moulding, usually found with a *fillet* on one or both sides.

Bore. The interior of a gun barrel, from the *chamber* forward to the muzzle.

Breech. The portion of a gun barrel from the rear end of the *chamber* aft to the *cascabel*.

Breech Ring. Also called *base ring*. A band of metal around the base of the *breech*.

Calibre. The diameter of a gun's bore.

Canister. Frequently called *case shot*, this short-range, antipersonnel ammunition was used as early as 1453 and continued in service as long as muzzle-loading artillery remained. A metal can, or case, contained iron or lead balls or metal scrap. Fired from a cannon, the container burst and scattered its pellets in the manner of an enormous shotgun. Canister did not have the longer-range effect of *grape*, but was more effective within a few hundred yards and replaced grape during the 1800s.

Carriage. The structure upon which the barrel of a gun, howitzer, or mortar was emplaced for use. Mortars were mounted on fixed wooden beds; howitzers used wheeled trail carriages which permitted relatively high elevation; guns used field or siege carriages with two large wheels and a trail, or were mounted on naval truck or military garrison carriages with four trucks (small wheels, usually less than 19inches diameter). On truck carriages the front trucks were slightly larger than the rear ones to allow for the camber of the ship's deck. Truck carriages were sometimes known as common standing carriages.

Carronade. A smoothbore, short range cannon designed and produced by the Carron Co. of Falkirk in Scotland. Known familiarly in the British service as 'the Smasher' and by enemies as the 'devil gun' it was designed to fire a heavy ball of low velocity.

Cascabel. Also spelled cascable; the rear of the gun barrel aft of the *breech ring*. It includes the *breech face* and the *cascabel button or pommelion*, the protrusion extending to the rear from the breech face. This knob was used as an attachment point for tackle when mounting or dismounting a piece from its carriage; breeching ropes used with naval guns to check their recoil were also attached to it.

Centre of metal. Notches on either side of muzzle and breech, used for levelling the gun.

Chamber. The rear end of a gun barrel, into which the powder charge was rammed when loading. Chambers of howitzers and mortars were usually smaller in diameter than the *bore*.

Chase. The portion of the barrel between the *reinforce(s)* and the *muzzle*. This was the thinnest portion of the gun barrel, since powder pressure was lower here than at the breech.

Elevating Screw. Vertical threaded shaft, its lower end rotating in a socket in a gun *carriage* and its upper end supporting the breech of the gun. A small cross-handle was attached to the upper end of the screw; as the gunner observed the target, he turned the screw handle to raise or lower the gun to the proper elevation. The elevating screw replaced the *quoin* in the 19th century.

Elevation. The difference between the axis of a gun's bore and the horizontal.

Fillet. Narrow, right-angled moulding, usually used in conjunction with an *astragal*.

Flintlock. On cannon, a firing mechanism which produced a shower of sparks by causing a flint to be struck against a frizzen (a roughened piece of metal). The sparks were directed down to ignite the main charge via an intermediary, which was either a gunpowder train or, in naval use, a quill tube. In the military the tube was made of tin packed with quickmatch. The term 'flintlock' is also used to describe a small arm employing that type of ignition system.

Fuze. A device used to explode the powder charge of a *shell*.

Gomer Chamber. Named after its inventor, a French officer. It consisted of a cone-shaped chamber at the breech end of the barrel, rounded at the end to concentrate the charge. Used in howitzers or shell guns it ensured that the projectile received the whole explosive force.

Grape. Also called *grapeshot* in some modern work; an antipersonnel projectile consisting of large iron shot grouped around an iron or wooden *stool* (a base disk supporting a vertical core), wrapped with cloth and tied into shape. A round of grape disintegrated when fired and scattered its fragments, and was widely used against troops during the 18th century before being replaced by *canister* during the 1800s. Its larger shot made it effective at longer ranges than canister, but it was less deadly at the critical shorter range.

Gun. A relatively long-barrelled artillery piece, firing its projectile at high velocities and flatter trajectories than the *howitzer* or *mortar*. This term is also sometimes used to refer to heavy ordnance fortifications, or for long-range firing.

Gunpowder. The propellant used in smoothbore cannon. Its origin is unknown. For some 500 years it was the only effective propellant. Known also as 'black powder' it consists of a mixture of charcoal, saltpetre and sulphur.

Gunport. An aperture in the ship's side through which a cannon was fired.

Handles. Rings, often stirrup-shaped but sometimes semicircular, cast in pairs on the upper side of gun and howitzer barrels at the centre of balance. With the *cascabel,* the handles were used to attach tackles when lifting a piece to or from its carriage. The handles of ornately decorated early ordnance were often cast in the form of dolphins, and early works call them by that name.

Handspike. Heavy wooden crowbar used to shift the trail of a gun *carriage* from side to side, or to raise the breech of the gun barrel so the *quoin* could be adjusted.

Howitzer. A weapon capable of firing shells at a high angle in order to engage targets sheltered from direct fire.

Line of Metal. A line drawn from the top of the base ring to the top of the muzzle.

Mortar. A short-barrelled weapon, sometimes cast integrally with its metal base and sometimes having a pair of *trunnions* at its breech end. Mortars were used in siege and bombardment work to "lob" explosive shells in a high, arching trajectory. Mortars did not have the mobility of the gun or the howitzer, but their ability to "drop" shells at high angles made them valuable siege and fortress weapons. Naval mortars were mounted in special "bomb vessels" and did not have to be picked up and moved from place to place; they were, thus usually longer and heavier than their land equivalents.

Muzzle. The opening at the forward end of the bore through which a piece is loaded. The flat forward portion of the gun barrel surrounding this is the *muzzle face.* The forward end of the gun barrel is often strengthened by a tulip-like enlargement called the *muzzle swell;* where a front sight, or *muzzle sight,* is used, this is mounted on the upper side of the swell. In some pieces, such as howitzers, a rectangular-shaped *muzzle band* is cast instead of a swell for reinforcement.

Muzzle Velocity. The speed, expressed in feet per second, of a projectile as it leaves the muzzle of a weapon.

Ogee. A moulding in the form of a reversed curve; that is, having a profile in the form of the letter S. An ogee is often used at the junction of two portions of a gun barrel with differing diameters, or it may be used with a *ring* as a *fillet* is used with an *astragal.*

Piece. A 'piece' of ordnance.

Point-blank. The range at which the projectile strikes the ground, or drops below the axis of the gun bore (the latter definition was often used with naval guns, mounted some distance above the water's surface), when the piece firing it is sighted along the *line of metal;* that is, directly along the upper line or the gun barrel from breech to muzzle. This was usually considered the effective shooting range, particularly for field or naval service, as compared to *random* firing.

Preponderance. The difference in weight between the breech end of a gun barrel, aft of its *trunnions*, and forward end.

Quoin. Wedge set beneath the breech of a gun and moved in or out to adjust elevation. It was eventually superseded by the *elevating screw*.

Racer Track, or 'Racers'. A curved track set into the floor of a gun emplacement which enabled the gun to be traversed.

Random. Term applied to ranges beyond *point-blank*, or to firing at such ranges. Accuracy of smoothbore artillery began to drop off sharply as a gun was elevated hence the very literal use of the word *random* in references to shooting at longer ranges. Because of this loss of accuracy, most gun carriages of this time did not permit more than a few degrees of elevation; howitzer carriages permitted somewhat more. The *quarter sights* on naval guns could elevate the gun three degrees, (by multiples of a quarter degree) as anything more could cause problems with the barrel striking the *gunport*.

Range. The horizontal distance between a gun and its target, or the distance at which a piece can hurl its projectile. In naval terminology ranges etc., ranges were roughly expressed in such terms as "pistol shot" (about 50yards); Fractions of these terms, such as "half- pistol shot", were also used.

Reinforce. The portion of the barrel between the *breech ring* and the *chase,* extending forward past the *trunnions*. Since powder pressure was greatest towards the breech, this part of the gun barrel was thicker than the chase. Howitzers and mortars had one reinforce, as did some guns. Other guns had two. The heavier breech reinforce is called the *first reinforce*, the lighter one, between the first reinforce and the chase, is the *second reinforce*.

Rifling. Arrangement of spiral *grooves* cut or cast into the bore of a piece to impart an axial spin to its projectile, thus giving it directional stability and greater accuracy. The raised sections between grooves are called *lands*, and the *calibre* of a rifled weapon is measured between opposite lands rather than groove to groove.

Rimbase. A stepped "shoulder" at the base of a *trunnion* where it joins the gun barrel. Not all trunnions had rimbases.

Ring. A rectangular moulding, sometimes used with an *ogee*.

Shell. An explosive projectile, made of cast iron filled with black powder. Smoothbore weapons fired spherical shells; rifled guns and some later smoothbores used elongated projectiles. Round shells used simple powder-train time *fuzes*. Since the direction of impact of a cylindrical rifled shell could be approximated, *fuzes* used in such rounds were also designed to detonate on impact.

Shot. A solid round projectile, of stone or cast iron, used in smoothbore muzzle-loading artillery.

Shrapnel. Frequently called *spherical-case shot*, this was an iron *shell* containing a number of *canister-* sized balls with a black-powder bursting charge and a powder-train time *fuze*. It was fired and exploded in the same manner as a conventional shell but when detonated scattered its small shot as well as the iron fragments of the shell itself. This ammunition was used by the British as early as 1808, but was not given its inventor's name until the 1850s. Shrapnel rounds were used in modern steel breechloading artillery well into the 20th century.

Sight. A device used to aim a *piece* at its target. These may be fixed or adjustable, and may be mounted over the centre line of the gun bore or offset to one side. High-angle mortars did not use sights; the wooden carriage of a mortar was first levelled, and the mortar was then aligned with the target with the help of a plumb line. The weight of the powder charge was varied to adjust the range.

Tangent Sight. A type of rear sight in which the length of the bar for any given elevation is equal to the tangent of that angle multiplied by the distance between the front and rear sights.

Touch Hole. The vent orifice. The hole at the top of the vent; the point at which the charge was fired (or 'touched off')

Trajectory. The curving path followed by a projectile from muzzle to target. *Guns* fired their shot at higher velocities, at relatively flatter trajectories, while low-velocity *mortars* had high trajectories.

Trunnion. Twin cylindrical projections, cast as part of a gun barrel and projecting to left and right at right angles to the bore, slightly forward of the centre of gravity. The trunnions supported the weight of the guns as it rested on its *carriage*, and the *piece* pivoted on them as it was raised or lowered in elevation. Placing trunnions forward of the centre of balance (3/7ths of the distance from breech to muzzle was an 18th century rule of thumb) placed the *preponderance* of barrel weight at the breech end and kept the *piece* stable when fired.

Tyres. There were two types of tyre in use, called the streak (or strake) tyre and the ring *tyre*. The streak tyre was in general use for all siege and field wheels until c.1868. It was formed of streaks (short lengths) of iron corresponding in number to the felloes in the wheel, each streak being secured to the felloes beneath by screw bolts and nails. The ring (or hoop) tyre was approved c.1868 for all wheels requiring a tyre of 3" or less in breadth. It was formed from a bar of hoop iron bent round and welded together, which after heating was shrunk on over the felloes, to which it was secured by nutted bolts, one through the middle of each felloe. (Le Mesurier p.14)

Vent. The narrow opening leading from the upper side of the *breech* to the after end of the *chamber*, used for igniting the powder charge to fire the *piece*. Earlier guns were primed with loose powder, and their vents are often surrounded by cup-shaped mouldings to receive powder. Later guns used priming tubes, and their vent openings are flush with the barrel. Hot powder gases are highly erosive, and the vents of guns were enlarged by repeated firing.

Windage. The difference between the bore diameter of a smoothbore artillery piece and the size of its shot or shell. Windage facilitated loading for the muzzle and allowed for black-powder fouling during firing as well as for irregularities in casting iron shot or forming stone ones. By the 18th century, windages were being standardised; the bores of English ordnance being made with a windage of 1/20 the diameter of their shot.

BIBLIOGRAPHY

ALL BOOKS PUBLISHED IN LONDON UNLESS OTHERWISE INDICATED

CONTEMPORARY DOCUMENTS

Royal Armouries – Tower of London
Blomefield Letter Books
Book 3   2: 11: 1786 –   2: 7: 1788
Book 4   8: 11: 1788 –   1: 9: 1790
Book 5   8: 8: 1790 – 17: 8: 1792
Royal Naval Museum – Portsmouth   Mss 118
[Standing] Order Books Capt. John Sutton HMS Egmont & HMS Superb 1798 – 1801
Naval Dispatches
London Gazette, May 18th 1782
London Gazette Extraordinary, November 6th 1805
RNM Mss 1998/41 Rivers Papers (Gunner's Log of *HMS Victory*)
RNM Mss 1986/573 (11) Journal of Midshipman Rivers
Chatham Dockyard
Admiralty Correspondence to Chatham Dockyard Commissioners 1712-1715
CDHS No. 13 *Master Attendants Letter Book*
CDHS No. 25A *Admiralty correspondence to Chatham Dockyard*
CDHS No. 25B *Admiralty Correspondence to Chatham Dockyard*
National Archives/Public Record Office – Kew
ADM2/225	Anson – Quarterdeck guns to be fitted with locks 21: 10: 1755
ADM2/261	HMS Woolwich – establishments for foreign and Channel service
ADM2/263	HMS Captain – no quarterdeck guns fitted 08: 11: 1755
ADM2/266	HMS Dreadnought – ditto later
SUPPLY 5/107	
18: 02: 1785	Capt. Fage reports on condition of guns
20: 02: 1785	Footnote – respective travel claims of labourers & artificers
13: 03: 1785	Screws in Matthews guns
17: 03: 1785	" " "
01: 08: 1785	Ref. to screws in French guns
26: 09: 1785	Exam. of guns at Portsmouth – mention of ring bulges
19: 08: 1786	Query ref. 'projection of metal similar to Pan'
21: 08: 1786	Dimensions and model of new pattern gun sent to Walker
24: 08: 1786	Insertion of screws in bores
02: 09: 1786	Comparison of Brass and Iron guns
07: 09: 1786	Quick-firing experiments – degree of heat
27: 11: 1786	Lord Howe – Loops on cascables approved – mention of Sir C. Douglas's method

11: 12: 1786   Loops removable if required – trials of felt sponge
29: 12: 1786   Instructions to Walker ref. loops
WO 47/108
20: 02: 1785   Screws in Matthews guns

BIBLIOGRAPHY (CONT'D)

WO 47/109
30: 01: 1787   Apparatus for water proof of guns (cf supply 5/107   11:12:1786 Sgt. Bell)
WO 47/109
01: 02: 1787   Working Hours in W. Indies
WO 51/4
04: 05: 1664   Cutting off Harp and Cross from Ordnance
SUPPLY 5/43
                 Drawings/dims. Of shells, fuzes, etc.
SUPPLY 5/49
22: 09: 1785   Capt. Fage's report from Portsmouth
10: 07: 1786   Office minutiae
17: 07: 1786   Walker comments on 18pdr. guns
15: 08: 1786   Attempt to further lighten 18pdr. guns
24: 08: 1786   Walker's receipt of draught of 32pdr. guns
11: 10: 1786   Walker's discovery of new casting method
30: 11: 1786   Walker/Lord Musgrave approve of new pattern gun
SHIP'S LOGBOOKS
ADM 51/285   Captain's Log H.M.S. Duke
ADM 52/1708   Master's Log H.M.S. Duke
ADM 51/365   Captain's Log H.M.S. Formidable
ADM 51/4193   Captain's Log H.M.S. Formidable
PERSONAL COLLECTIONS
The J.D. Moody Collection (Ordnance Drawings donated to Central Library Portsmouth)

BIBLIOGRAPHY – SECONDARY SOURCES

BAILEY, SARAH B. *Prince Rupert's Patent Guns.*
Royal Armouries 2000

BLACKMORE, H.L. *The Armouries of the Tower of London Pt. 1 Ordnance.* H.M.S.O 1976

BURKES GENERAL ARMOURY Pub. Edward Churton 1842

CARUANA, A.B. *The History of English Sea Ordnance 1523-1875 Vol I 1994*
The History of English Sea Ordnance 1523 – 1875 Vol II 1995
Boudriot Pubs. Rotherfield

CHANT, COLIN (Ed.) *Science, Technology and Everyday Life 1870-1950*
Open Univ. 1989

CHARTRAND, RENÉ See Osprey Pubs.

CLEERE H. & CROSSLEY, D. *The Iron Industry of the Weald*
Leicester 1985 University Press.

CROWDY, TERRY See Osprey Pubs.

DOUGLAS, GEN. SIR HOWARD *A Treatise on Naval Gunnery 1855*
John Murray 1855

ELVIN, MAJ. J.G.D. *British Gunfounders 1700-1855*
Greenwich 1983
Handbook of the 32pdr. Smooth Bore Cannon 1805
Published privately

FFOULKES *Gunfounders of England*
Arms and Armour Press

HENRY, CHRIS See Osprey Pubs.

HOWARTH, DAVID *A Brief History of British Sea Power*
Robinson 2003

HUGHES, BASIL PERRONET *British Smooth-Bore Artillery*
Arms and Armour 1969

HODGKINSON, JEREMY		*The Wealden Iron Industry* The History Press Port Stroud, Glos. 2008
HOGG, IAN V & JOHN BATCHELOR		*Naval Gun* Blandford Press Poole 1978
HOGG, IAN V.		*The Illustrated Encyclopaedia of Ammunition* Quantum 2003
JACKSON, M.H. & DE BEER		*18th Century Gunfounding* David and Charles Newton Abbot 1973
KENNARD, A.N.		*Guns and Gunfounding* Arms and Armour 1986
MAC.KINNON, CHARLES		*The Observer's Book of Heraldry* Fred Warne. Fred Warne & Co. 1966
LLOYD, E.W. & HADCOCK, A.G		*Artillery. Its progress and Present Position* J. Griffin & Co. Portsmouth 1893
MEHL, HANS.		*Naval Guns.* Chatham Pub. 2002
MESURIER, LE. Capt. Cecil B.		*Notes on the Manufactures of the Royal Carriage Dept. 1868.* HMSO 1868. D.P&G. 2006
MOORE, DAVID		*A Handbook of Military Terms* Pub. Palmerston Forts. Soc. Fareham 1966
MOORE, D & SALTER, G.		*Mallet's Great Mortars* Palmerston Forts Society, Fareham.
MUNDAY, JOHN		*Naval Cannon* Shire Pubs. Aylesbury 1987

OSPREY PUBS. LTD. OXFORD

HENRY, CHRIS	2002	*British Napoleonic Artillery 1793-1815* (1) Field Artillery
HENRY, CHRIS	2003	*British Napoleonic Artillery 1793-1815* (2) Siege and Coastal Artillery
HENRY, CHRIS	2004	*Napoleonic Naval Armaments 1792-1815*

CHARTRAND, RENÉ	2003	
	2003	(a) *Napoleon's Guns 1792-1815 (1)* Field Arty. (b) *Napoleon's Guns 1792-1815 (2)* Heavy and Siege Arty.
CROWDY, TERRY	2005	*French Warship Crews 1789-1805*
PATTERSON, B.H.		*Guns of Portsmouth* Fort Cumberland & Portsmouth Militaria Soc.
SMITH, ROBERT. D. (Ed.)		*British Naval Armaments* Royal Armouries 2004
SMITH, R.D. & R.R. BROWN		*Bombards. Mons Meg and her Sisters* Royal Armouries 1989
STRAKER, E.		*Wealden Iron* Pub. Bell 1931
WATTERS, BRIAN		*Where Iron Runs Like Water. A New History of Carron Iron Works 1759-1982* John Donald Pubs. Edinburgh

BIBLIOGRAPHY – SECONDARY SOURCES (CONT'D)

REPORTS

BAKER, H.A.	*The Crisis in Naval Ordnance 1983* NMM No. 56 OUP

DICTIONARIES

MATTHEW, H.C.G & BRIAN HARRISON (Eds.) WORKMAN. B.A. (Ed.)	*Oxford Dictionary of National Biography* *The New Caxton Encyclopeadia* OU Press Caxton 1969